KEEPERS OF THE TREASURE

Love & Blessings!
John Summers

KEEPERS OF THE TREASURE

CREATE A GODLY HERITAGE

JoAn Summers

PRAYER MOUNTAIN PRESS
P.O. BOX 210733   DALLAS, TEXAS 75211

KEEPERS OF THE TREASURE

Scripture quotations are from
The Holy Bible, New International Version
by Zondervan Bible Publishers,
Grand Rapids, Michigan 49506, USA.

ISBN: 0-9657997-0-0

Published by:
Prayer Mountain Press
5950 Eagle Ford Drive
Dallas, Texas 75249

Mailing Address:
P. O. Box 210733
Dallas, Texas 75211

Cover Design by David Harper
Back Cover Photo by Deby Dearman
Printed in the United States of America

Robert and JoAn Summers, Pastors
5950 Eagle Ford Drive Dallas, Texas 75249
(972) 296-8919   Fax (972) 709-7313
email: mtcreek@aol.com   internet: www.mtcreek.com

DEDICATION

To my mother, Eva Darst Holder,

A lady who loves her Lord and her family,

With gratitude for the Godly heritage she gave me,

Which I treasure,

And

To my granddaughters, my precious ones,

Mackenzie Grace and Riley Olivia Summers,

With love and prayers that this Godly heritage

Which I pass on to them will become their treasure as well.

CONTENTS

Glean wisdom for raising children from four key areas:
love, guidance, discipline, and instruction in righteousness.
Grow in grace. Grow in practical wisdom. Find practical,
easy-to-apply solutions to common problems.

Gain a new understanding of discretion. Use words as
instruments of healing. Explore the practical out-workings
of discretion. Preserve dignity. Hear beyond words.
Manifest a gentle, quiet spirit.

Enrich your marriage. Enter into the guilt-free pleasures
of God-ordained passion. Enjoy intimacy within the security
of a lifetime partnership. Hear practical counsel on issues
from the bedroom to the bankbook. Seek wisdom for
raising pure young people in a polluted world.

Chapter Ten

HOME IS WHERE THE HEART IS
Matthew 6:21
For where your treasure is, there your heart will be also.   233

Discover the hidden treasures of your family. Pass along
a priceless heritage. Recognize and utilize these treasures,
as you celebrate the gifts of the heart. Cultivate your family's
particular legacy. Build eternity into the daily routines of life.

CHAPTER 1

KEEPERS AT HOME

"That they may teach the young women"
Titus 2:4

Two lively third-graders, Jennifer and Patti, come skipping up the sidewalk. Their bouncing curls and prancing ponytails show joy at release from the confining classroom. However, for Patti this walk is only a brief respite of freedom. She has explicit instructions to go straight home every day, unlock the door, then relock and bolt it behind her. Once inside, she must call Mother at work to report getting home safely. After that, she will fill the lonely hours until her parents arrive in whatever way she can.

Patti is part of a growing segment in our modern society called "latchkey children." A latchkey child has no mother waiting to welcome her home. No one greets her with a hug, praises the first pastel drawing she made in art class, or listens to the funny new song she learned. Mother is at her post in the city government office. Dad is dictating another sales report to his secretary. They have both assured Patti that she is a big girl, responsible enough to carry the housekey on a little chain around her neck. Hence the name "Latchkey Child."

After shutting herself in, Patti usually grabs a Twinkie or Pudding Pop, cuddles her frayed, stuffed bunny, and settles down in front of the television. This is her daily routine. She has no choice but to accept the decisions made by her parents. One time she queried her mother as to why she could not stay home "like Jennifer's mom does." Mother patiently, painstakingly explained. "Patti, I'm different from Jennifer's mom. I need a career to be fulfilled. I have a bright mind that needs the challenge of the political scene. Honey, I would feel trapped if I had to stay at home. And besides," she smiled, brushing back Patti's curls, "how else will we ever save enough money for your trip to Disneyworld if I don't work?" But Patti's mind had hung on the word *trapped*. That described exactly how she feels every day when she comes home.

A NOTE ON THE FRIDGE

Mike Williams comes swirling into his driveway, jumps out of his car, and hits the front door in three long strides. Face beaming a triumphant smile, hand clutching a bouquet of daisies, he throws open the door. "Honey, I did it! I got the contract!" he yells. "Come on, let's go celebrate!"

Silence meets him. From room to room he searches excitedly. "Lisa, honey, did you hear me? I won! Lisa? Where are you?" His eyes spy the hastily written note on the refrigerator door: Mike, Mr. Hastings called asking me to show that property again. I'm taking the client to dinner. Just grab a sandwich or something, okay?

Joy plummets. Anger rises. "Great, just great," Mike fumes, tossing the bright flowers in a heap on the floor. "That's three, no, four times this week. Some part-time job."

Mike needs someone to share and celebrate his moment of triumph. Disappointed by his wife's absence, he may find someone else to admire his victory. This is not a conscious decision on his part, for Mike has always been a faithful husband. But right now he has an emotional need and his wife is not there to fill it. Nor has she been there for him on several recent occasions.

As Mike walks into the bar of his favorite restaurant, he is surprised to see Anita, a cheerleader from his old high school days. She is recently divorced, delighted to see Mike again, more than willing to share fun memories over dinner. And she certainly knows how to cheer Mike's triumph today.

UNTAPPED WISDOM

Eighty year old Kate stares out the window of her small efficiency apartment. Another day is ending. Another sunset. A lingering beam of light plays across her soft white hair, creating a halo effect. Faded blue eyes wreathed with wrinkles look vacantly into the long, empty hours stretched before her. "One can only sleep so much," she murmurs, "even a tired old body like me."

Played out against the deepening hues of the evening sky, Kate's thoughts bring a smile. She remembers her happier days, "when I was useful, when my life counted for something."

In truth, this lady's life could still be useful if she were integrated into a family. She is a reservoir of untapped wisdom which only years of living can impart. But her two daughters have no place for her in their homes. They are far too busy, too upwardly mobile, doing too much entertaining to have Mother around poking into things. How trying it is to them when she starts in on one of her Do-you-remember tales. Yet they think she is too frail and forgetful to live alone anymore. They decided she should be in a place where she could have around-the-clock care.

So, lonely Kate has been installed in a spanking new, color-coordinated, high-rise retirement complex far away from the home and neighborhood she holds dear. The two daughters think her ungrateful because she is not thrilled to live in this place where she never has to lift a finger. "After all, Mother, this place is not cheap!" They cannot seem to understand that starting all over, making new friends, adjusting to a new bed, having strangers check on you all the time is quite difficult to accept when you are old and settled in your ways.

She has learned to keep her complaints tucked away, evidenced only by gentle sighs. She simply sits by her window, careworn hands folded idly in her lap, smiling softly at a memory, one of her Do-you-remember tales.

PASSING THE FLAME OF LOVE AND STABILITY

How will little Patti ever grow into a nurturing keeper at home when she has no example to guide her, no pattern to follow? How long will Mike and Lisa's marriage hold together if they continue to grow farther apart emotionally? How long will Grandmother Kate's life continue when she has already been made to feel useless?

These are three examples I have drawn from many years of observing and counseling brokenhearted people. You probably know someone who fits into one of these three scenes. Perhaps you see yourself.

Our world today has a crying need for keepers at home. This cry comes from families shattering into heartbreak, from children uprooted and tossed onto sullen emotional seas. It is the cry of spiritual wanderers who have lost all faith. The lonely, longing cry of those who know *home* as only some distant illusion.

It is time to heed this cry. Women today must become keepers at home in this homeless world.

Mothers today must begin to realize that children are gifts given by God. They are immortal souls He has created and entrusted to our care. No day care center in the world will love and train our children the way God intended us to do. Our children need keepers at home.

Wives today must begin to realize that it takes time and energy and emotional effort to make a marriage work. A happy home does not just fall together. If we spend ourselves on an uncaring marketplace, coming home exhausted at day's end, what do we have left to give our husbands? They need loving keepers at home.

Daughters of elderly parents must begin to realize that shunt-

6

ing them aside for other ambitions is a direct violation of God's Fifth Commandment, "Honor your father and mother." It also deprives grandchildren and great-grandchildren of their root system: that invaluable connection of seeing life's continuity stretch from last century down through this century into next century. From one keeper to the next, passing the flame of love and stability along through the generations.

Keepers at home. How succinct is God's Word. How much to the point. The finger of God writes in one short phrase what is the inner yearning of every wife and mother, to be a *keeper at home*. (Titus 2:5 KJV) This means far more than "just a housewife," a term which the world ridicules with a patronizing sneer. She is even more than a homemaker.

A keeper at home is a woman who has accepted the calling of God on her life to minister to her husband and her children, deeming this the most worthy, honorable profession she can name. She makes her home a secure place of peace and rest. She weaves the fabric of the family together so that no external stress can tear it apart. She pleases the heart of her husband and keeps him in love and loving through the ups and downs of life. She blesses her children with stability, an unshakable belief that *home* means goodness and godliness, a firm foundation for framing their own lives.

A keeper at home is the kind of woman who comes to mind when someone tries to depict an ideal mother. We have all known ladies like this. Who comes to your mind? Is she an older woman? Today most keepers at home belong to the generation born before World War II, before fathers became fighters and mothers filled defense factories.

WHERE ARE THE KEEPERS?

Looking around at the wives and mothers who people our world today, we find precious few for whom keeping a home is a priority. In fact, it startled D. L. Stewart, the columnist who writes the syndicated

"Paternity Ward" to note that full-time motherhood has become such a curiosity it rated a feature story on his local six o'clock newscast. About this particular story, Mr. Stewart posed some penetrating observations: "Something makes me wonder why it is necessary to take a camera into a woman's home and ask her to explain her reasons for staying home all day and caring for her children . . . Has the world changed so much that there's no longer room for a woman who feels it's important for a ten-year-old to know that there will be someone waiting at home who really wants to hear about all the good things that happened to-day? And all the bad things. Who decided there's no satisfaction in holding a crying child on her lap and kissing away the tears?"

Who indeed?

THE GREAT LIE

The majority of women themselves have made this choice because they have swallowed the deceptive bait of what I call "The Great Lie." The feminist movement, aided and abetted by the media, has dangled a tantalizing lure of "independence from men" and "female power" before a nation of spiritually starved women. They snapped it up hungrily and are now caught on the hook of their own choices.

The Great Lie goes like this: "Women can no longer be kept in their place at home, for we are strong and proud and invincible. We can do anything and everything. We can be a powerful executive in the marketplace all day, a quality mother in the evening when we get home, and an exciting lover to our husbands at night. We need all this to be fulfilled!" Helen Gurley Brown's bestseller "Having It All" is based on this premise.

If indeed the premise is true, why are marriages fracturing at an unparalleled rate? If quality mothering can be done in a few minutes each evening, why are today's children so rebellious that many schools resemble armed camps? Why are teenagers and even young children growing so desperate as to take their own lives in increasing numbers each year?

If we choose the lifestyle of The Great Lie, when do we have time to replenish our own souls, moments for the quiet times we need so much to keep peace and tranquility in our families? Yes, you may know someone who seems to be keeping all these balls juggled in the air right now—but for how long? Why is there a growing phenomenon of runaway mothers today?

Once I was asking just such questions as these on a national radio program "Point of View." As I challenged the prevailing views of the feminist movement, host Marlin Maddoux wryly commented, "I'll bet Betty Friedan loves you!"

A NEW SET OF PROBLEMS

The truth is, even devout feminists such as Friedan are asking themselves tough questions about this movement they helped to create. In her book *The Second Stage*, Friedan realistically shows that the new opportunities, the new options and choices have created a whole new set of problems. The theory of having it all, dynamic career, understanding husband, brilliant children, is not easily attained in the reality of day to day living.

A real life case in point is the beautiful Ivana Trump. This lovely lady suffered incredible public humiliation as her husband's rejection and infidelity were splattered across tabloid headlines for weeks. Somehow she kept her poise and dignity. In a televised interview she was asked this crucial question about having it all — the marriage, the children, the glamorous career. She responded poignantly, "I think a woman can have it all. But perhaps, not all at the same time."

In her best-selling book *Passages*, Gail Sheehy has this to say about the women who try to do it all. "Integrators," she calls them. "Marriage did not stop us from working toward accomplishment, nor did childbirth, although it usually caused us to slow down . . . We were determined not to end up as the hard-boiled career woman stereotype, or as the forgotten drunks at the other end of our husbands' commuter line . . . And most of us didn't. We found ourselves coming out somewhere else and passed into our thirties with a different crisis. Something had to go."

"Most integrators subtracted the marriage, or gave up on the career, or let the children go to hell." (pp. 276-277, E. P. Dutton & Co.)

So many women who swallowed The Great Lie find themselves unable to cope with all the demands upon them in year after year reality. They wind up with the rejection of a failed marriage. Or they bring up children who are little more than strangers to them. Generally they choose to sacrifice their personal lives on the altar of the career they have built. That is the rallying cry of the feminist movement: "We must not give up any ground we have gained in the business world, no matter what the cost. We hold the future of all women in our hands."

I am here to proclaim that you do not have to respond to the pressure of today's world. It is imperative to realize that the world's standard for living is *not* a biblical standard. You do not have to accept the guilt that the world dishes out.

THE LIE FROM THE FATHER OF LIES

The Great Lie which deceives women today is belched forth from the very pit where every lie originates, from Satan who is the father of lies. His purpose is to seek and destroy God's precious creations. (I Peter 5.8) Satan has no scruples. He rips people to shreds. He chews them up physically and emotionally. His fiendish laughter echoes through the divorce courts as he leaves broken bits and pieces of families strewn around. Do not believe him. Do not sacrifice your home and husband and children and peace of mind to follow his wicked

10

lie. Always remember that the thief comes only to steal and to kill and to destroy.

But there is hope!

Jesus Christ came to give you life, more abundant life than you ever dreamed. (John 10.10) Follow His ways. Search out His pattern for your life. Become a Kingdom woman who can see things through the focus of the Kingdom of God rather than the filter of the world. Listen to the good counsel God has for you, rather than heeding the siren of the world which leads only to despair. Choose life!

Life is a series of choices, day after day. If you are a woman who chooses to pursue a career instead of opting for husband and children, you have every right to do so. That may be God's perfect plan for your life. You may be the woman who discovers the cure for cerebral palsy. Perhaps you will influence thousands of lives for good as a teacher. You may be the banker who gives wise counsel and the wherewithal to turn failure into success for struggling businessmen. Hundreds of options are open to you. And if that is your choice, I say, "Go for it!" Be the very best you can be. Those of us who have chosen differently will admire your success, but we will not be envious. For we all make our own choices.

If in the midst of your successful career you find yourself falling in love with a man, wanting to marry him, create a home for him, and bear his children, you will face a most difficult choice. Marriage, husband, children cannot—will not—be simply an addendum to your already full lifestyle. You will be facing the exchange of one career for another—just as worthy, just as honorable.

A HOME, A HUSBAND, TWO KIDS AND A CAT

Pat is a beautiful, poised, successful banker. Her determination in banking school with all those men was to rise to the top of her profession as quickly as possible. For her that meant being offered the presidency of her own bank. Only thirty-seven years old, Pat is now

11

the senior vice-president of a burgeoning new bank. Her goal is within sight. She told me rather wistfully, "It really doesn't matter anymore. I know I can do it. But my priorities have changed." When I inquired about those changes, she said, "I want a home, a faithful husband who loves me, two kids and a cat."

One of my dearest friends and one of God's finest women is the delightful Elizabeth Brown. Remaining single all her young adult life, she served fifteen years in the hotel industry. She resolutely climbed the corporate ladder with all its accompanying stress and was determined to make it in a man's world. Then she fell in love with a charming widower who had two little girls. Elizabeth stepped out of the business realm into the home and hearts of three people to whom death had dealt a heavy blow. She brought laughter and life and love to them. Her sparkle dispelled the gloom. Home once again held a wife and mother. Though her life changed radically, and those changes were not without some pain, Elizabeth has never regretted her choice.

GOD'S CREATIVE SOLUTIONS

Obviously I am speaking here to women who do have a choice. Unfortunately there are far too many women who no longer have the liberty of choice. Those whose husbands have been incapacitated by tragedy or illness are compelled to earn the living, whether they like it or not. Many lovely homemakers lost the liberty of choice when, for whatever reason, their husbands walked out, shattered the marriage covenant, and dishonored God and family.

If you are in such a place, please realize that God's grace will cover you. He is your Provider, your security. Honor His Kingdom principles of tithing and giving and good stewardship. Integrate yourself into a loving church family where you will receive both physical help and spiritual covering. Seek the Lord for a way out of your dilemma. Perhaps He will lead you into a cottage industry where you could work at home. Check out Work-at-Home sourcebooks from your library.

For His faithful children, our Father has creative solutions to problems which seem completely insurmountable. If you truly long to be a keeper at home for your children, make Psalm 37:4,5 your plan for living: "Delight yourself in the Lord and he will give you the desires of your heart. Commit your way to the Lord; trust in him and he will do this." Delight in Him. Trust in Him. He sees the desire of your heart.

A "HIGHER" STANDARD OF LIVING?

Most mothers who work outside their home do so because they want a higher standard of living than their husband can provide. One salary does not go far enough to satisfy them.

Truly the "Me Generation" concept has taken firm root in today's thinking. Rather than choosing to serve their husbands and children, seeing them as gifts of God to be treasured, women are increasingly saying, "Me first. If there is any time left over, my family can have it." This line of action is based on another rampant lie from the pit which declares, "It's not the quantity of time you spend with your family, it's the *quality* of time. When you have less time, you make it count for more."

QUALITY VS QUANTITY

A renowned family psychologist, Dr. James Dobson, responds to this prevailing notion: "If quantity and quality are worthwhile ingredients in family relationships, then why not give our kids both? ... My concern is that the quantity-versus-quality cliche has become, perhaps, a rationalization for giving our kids neither! This phrase has been bandied about by over-committed and harassed parents who feel guilty about the lack of time they spend with their children. Their boys and girls are parked at childcare centers during the day and with babysitters at night, leaving little time for traditional parenting activities. And to handle the discomfort of neglecting their children, Mom and Dad cling to a catch phrase that makes it seem so healthy and proper: 'Well, you know, it's not the quantity of time that matters, it's the quality of your togetherness that counts.' I maintain that this convenient generalization simply won't hold water." (p. 27, *Dr. Dobson Answers Your Questions*, Tyndale House Publishers)

YOUR PRECIOUS POSITION

Christian women must realize the preciousness of their position as keepers at home. Precious in value. Precious in number. We are fast becoming an endangered species as the ideology of this present world encroaches into the Kingdom of God. Keep in mind that Jesus Christ is our example, not the media stars we see daily. God's Word is our guide, not the flashy magazines or bold billboards touting "You've come a long way, Baby." And His Word clearly states, "Whoever practices and teaches these commands will be called great in the kingdom of heaven." (Matthew 5:19b) A little later He explained true greatness in this way, "Whosoever will be great among you, let him be your minister; and whosoever will be chief among you, let him be your servant: even as the Son of man came not to be ministered unto, but to minister, and to give his life a ransom for many." (Matthew 20:26-28 KJV)

You can see how far this world's concept of greatness has strayed from God's Kingdom greatness. I urge you to follow His plan for greatness! Serve your family joyfully and see what fulfillment it brings to be recognized as a great woman of God. Your children will rise up and call you "Blessed!" and your husband also will praise you. (See Proverbs 31:28)

One of the loveliest compliments I ever received was a scribbled note left for me one day by Rod Butler, the young man who lived with us for almost two years. In that time he learned how a family works. Simple gratitude for everyday kindness spilled out onto a piece of scratch paper:

"Jo," he wrote, "a thank you has been welling up in me–and here it is. Thank you for a warm family home which I call my own. Thank you for leftovers, saran wrapped in the fridge, which speak care & thoughtfulness. Not to mention chocolate chip cookies. Thank you for serving me freedom & love, and thanks for your support. With all the buzzing we do, your soft touch keeps the house a home–brings a sense of family, acceptance, belonging, & peace. I wonder how you do all that . . . A woman's way? Could be. All this to say: You're special. I'm grateful. And even if I don't always say so, *I love you!* – Rod"

That little scrap of paper is precious to me. My spiritual son Rod rose up and called me "Blessed!"

TRUE KINGDOM GREATNESS

Serving others. Loving them. Being the arms of Jesus to hold them when they hurt. Making a safe place they can run to when they need help. Serving warm cookies and milk to a tough, smartmouthed teenager who needs an example of grace in his life. Washing the sheets and making the bed yet another time for the unexpected guest who needs a place of peace for a night or two. Teaching a young lady who never learned any feminine skills how to set the table, how to can tomatoes, how to remove spots from her dress. Sharing a favorite poem which suits the occasion. Offering tea and comfort. Serving others. Loving them. Being an example of Jesus in their lives.

This is true Kingdom greatness. It takes time and energy and effort.

Very few women have the stamina to work outside the home all day, then still have energy and time left for anything except the immediate, pressing needs of their own household. How can they be

15

Jesus to the world? There is no time, no energy even to care.

Most brides who have a career choose to continue working until they begin their family. Allow me to offer a word of caution. Decide now to live on your husband's income. Set yours aside to use for some specific goal, such as furniture purchase or down payment on a home. Discipline yourself to daily living on only one income. That way, when you leave the job force to have your baby, your standard of living will already be established. You will not be jolted by a pile of unpaid bills into dropping Baby at the nearest daycare center in order to get that second paycheck coming in again.

DELUDED AND DESTROYED

Sometimes after the children are grown and gone, women decide to go back to work simply because they are bored or lonely. There is a real danger here. Often these women get so caught up in the excitement of a new career they begin to neglect that primary relationship of husband/wife.

I watched in growing dismay as one pastor's beautiful wife became more and more involved in a burgeoning real estate career. She began to make money hand over fist. She wined and dined prospective clients at exclusive restaurants. She pampered herself with luxuries she had never known on a pastor's salary. She became fascinated with her glamorous, freewheeling boss. Up to that time she had always been a vital part of her husband's ministry. But he and the church grew to be dull, boring to her. Finally this lovely lady was completely deluded by the lust of this world. She deserted her husband, stunned the church, wrecked her godly reputation, and almost destroyed her son when he reeled away in drunken despair.

Our choices. How desperately important they are.

In addition to living in the reality of the choices we make, we must recognize the changing *seasons* of our lives. Just as each passing year follows a certain progression, so does the general pattern of our lives.

SPRING AND SUMMER

In the springtime freshness of youth, we establish the root systems that will nurture us all our lives. Our long years of schooling finally culminate in a release to the wide world of opportunity. At least, that is what we hear at every graduation ceremony. We begin a career and establish our independence from our parents. A season has passed, a new one begins.

About this time our true love appears and we make joyful plans to be a beautiful bride. Spring turns into the lushness of summer with trees and gardens growing, bright hot days of happy vacation wanderings, lemonade and watermelon stands beckoning. Our careers set aside, we begin creating new life with our husbands. We thrill to our son's appearance on the scene of our lives. We sag under the weight of bottles, diapers, feedings, changes, even as we are blessed with a little brother for Baby and another unplanned little sister. Remember, young mother, seasons pass all too soon.

AUTUMN AND WINTER

All the growth of summertime culminates in autumn's brisk harvest time. How quickly our children grow up and away from us. Autumn sends them away to school, to football games and drill teams, then to the University or their own career. How proud we are to see the little lives we have nurtured turn out to be strong, godly young men and women. Our harvest is bountiful.

Another season passes, this time turning into winter. It has been called "The Empty Nest Syndrome," this earliest stage of winter. We can allow it to chill us and make us brittle, or we can rekindle the fires that have dampened down through the years. This is the season to rejoice in these lines from Robert Browning.

> Grow old along with me!
> The best is yet to be,
> The last of life, for which the first was made.
> Our times are in his hand
> Who saith, A whole I planned;
> Youth shows but half. Trust God; see all,
>   nor be afraid!

This is the season to do all those things with your husband that you never had the time or energy or funds for during the demands of parenting. Winter is wonderful! Think of the holiday time and all the joy it brings: love, sparkle, gifts, grandchildren, friends, memories. All these are vital parts of your winter season. Enjoy it to its fullest. Although you no longer have the springtime blossom of youth or the bountiful energy of summertime or the abundance of autumn, yet your winter season is a blessed time to cherish.

ONE SEASON AT A TIME

Sometimes we tend to overlap our seasons. That creates added stress, as I discovered when I overlapped the "new bride" season on top of the "college student" season. Professors' demands to be met. Husband's needs and desires to be fulfilled. Laundry and meals and planning. Increased financial worries. Forget that old saw about two living as cheaply as one; it simply cannot be done! Only lots of love and Jesus got me through that time of overlapping seasons.

All my life my besetting sin has been trying to do too many things at one time until I stretched myself to the snapping point. Sure enough, right after graduation I jumped into a fulltime teaching career, while trying to build our nest, trying to help Robert salvage the lives of the inner city children he taught, and trying to be a blessing to my family, friends, and church. In the summertime, instead of taking a much needed rest, I drove all over the Houston area establishing Vacation Bible Clubs for children. Even the increasing nausea of pregnancy did not stop me.

ANYTHING HE ASKS OF ME

When my son was born, after a difficult pregnancy, I felt blessed beyond words. A whole new season of my life had begun. But I could not regain my strength and energy. Pain mounted each day, racking my nerves and body. In six short weeks I was back in the hospital for major surgery. Mother had to take my infant son home with her. I sobbed bitterly over the whole turn of events. Why, after enduring a stressful pregnancy, after yearning for this child, why was I not even strong enough to care for him? Right there in that hospital bed I really began to focus on the importance of fulltime wife and mother. Forget the career. Who needs graduate school? "God, forgive me for fitting everything I wanted in ahead of my time with You and my husband."

You see, I had balked at Robert's desire to enter ministry. I had stubbornly refused that kind of lifestyle. Now there I was, flat on my back, spiritually spent, emotionally drained, physically exhausted. Lying there in the hospital unable to do anything but think, I entered a major attitude adjustment time.

Robert was in his own crucible, for he could not rest until he responded to the calling of God on his life. But he loved me too much to leave me behind while he forged on ahead. One evening at my bedside he broached the subject of entering ministry again. At long last I turned my selfish will over to God. I took the plunge into unknown waters. Looking steadfastly at my precious husband, I vowed, "If God will get me out of this hospital bed and make me well and strong so that I can hold you and my baby in my arms again, I will do anything, go anywhere, be anything He asks of me."

The Living God heard me and took me at my word. He made a covenant of health with me that evening. I began to improve steadily from that moment. Within one week, I was home from the hospital, my baby was back in my arms, my life was coming into order, my grateful husband was charting our new course of action for the future.

That was over thirty years ago. Never once in the intervening years have I been back in the hospital nor have I been plagued by any serious health problems. I have kept my side of the covenant too. Whatever the Lord has asked, I have diligently tried to do. He has led me into an exciting, fulfilling life, through an incredible variety of experiences. I am sure there is still more to come than I have ever asked or dreamed. Never have I regretted my choice to put Him and Robert first.

A NEW PLACE TO BEGIN

You may be reading this and thinking, "That sounds great for you, but what about me? My life is a hopeless, tangled mess. My husband doesn't love me anymore. He hardly even notices I'm here. My kids are rebellious and smartmouthed. They're out doing God-knows-what right now. Nobody really likes me, including myself. I'd shove my resignation under my boss's nose tomorrow if I could, but we've got bills stacked up to there. So it's too late for me."

My friend, please don't lose hope. I have a promise for you, one which is eternally true: Our God always gives us a new place to begin. He is the God of new beginnings. No matter how tangled the threads of our lives, He sees the end from the beginning and knows just how to pull the right strings to straighten things out.

The first and foremost step toward wholeness is to accept Jesus Christ as Savior, Redeemer, and Lord of your life. Without Him, all is lost. With Him, everything is new. "If any man be in Christ, he is a new creature; old things are passed away; behold, all things are become new." (II Corinthians 5:17 KJV) If this is what you need — a fresh start on life — a new beginning, do not hesitate. Right now ask Christ Jesus to clean up your life and make you whole. He redeems our life from sin and destruction. That is why we call Him our Redeemer.

When we call Him our Lord, we mean that we give Him the right to rule our lives. Hear His promise to you in Jeremiah 29.11, "For I know the plans I have for you, declares the Lord, plans to prosper you and not to harm you, plans to give you a hope and a future."

A BRIGHT NEW TOMORROW

A future and a hope. Trust Him with your future. He brings hope for a bright new tomorrow. He gives us principles to live by that really *do* work. Remember, this choice to accept or reject Jesus Christ is the most important choice you will ever make. Every future action you take will reflect this life or death choice. Please choose life!

All the principles which can bring you into a happy new beginning are written in God's Word, His handbook for living. If it is difficult for you to understand the Bible, find some good books and Bible study classes to help you. Most important, find a Body of believers to guide you, a church home and family.

JEWELS FOR LIVING

I hope you will learn in these pages how to see your life through God's Kingdom focus. Let's hold up God's standard as set forth in His Word. Let's take our rightful places as daughters of the King. Let's choose to honor our King by living our lives in an honorable way.

The principles He sets forth in Titus 2 have been completely

21

buried by the world view we have heard all our lives. Come help me mine these lost treasures, polish and present them once more as jewels for living.

Our Heavenly Father expects this kind of behavior from us:
to be sober,
to love our husband,
to love our children,
to be discreet,
to be chaste,
to be keepers at home,
to be good,
and finally, to be obedient to our own husband.
These are God's directions for us, His principles for living. They do work. They must be learned and followed.

I long to show you what a privilege it is to be a keeper of the treasure. What a joy and delight. What a worthy and honorable position it is. I hope you will see how important you are in the tapestry of life and love our God is weaving.

ETERNAL RICHES

Keepers of the treasure are women who know the true values of this life. Love. Hope. Faith. Family. Beauty. Courage. Grace. All these are enduring riches which will last eternally.

How do we get them?

How to we keep them?

How do we become the kind of person Perry Tankley describes in this wonderful poem:

If all the music died
And music makers ceased,
I think you'd stand and sing
A hymn of hope and peace.

If might of doubt and fear
Against the Light were hurled,
I think you'd light a candle
And stand against the world.

If winds of changing times
Uprooted trees and sod,
I think instead of mocking
You'd stand in praise of God.

The beauty of your life
Is like a work of art
Inscribed by Memory's hand
Upon my grateful heart.

—Perry Tankley, 1986

If this is a picture of who you want to be, then come walk with me through the following pages as I share with you the treasures of my heart.

CHAPTER 2

SEEING CLEARLY

"to be sober"
Titus 2:4

O n the evening of a recent Palm Sunday, my television broad-
cast with unintentional irony the muddled mindset of modern
man. That day is so clear to me because our church family had
just celebrated the triumphal entry of Christ as King with worship and
singing and picnicking in Dallas' historic Old City Park. We ate at the
bountifully laden tables. We basked in love and sunshine. Teens
romped with toddlers beneath blue skies and scudding clouds. Older
folks watched and smiled and swapped tales. Good cooks gathered to
exchange recipes and perhaps have "one last bite" of Eva's cornbread
dressing or Nina's taco salad. Joyous sounds from "Cloudburst," our
young people's music group, wafted out across the green grass spread
with patchwork quilts. A visiting French family of tourists wandered
through and was brought in to share the delightful American custom of
dinner on the grounds. It was a lovely time of togetherness.

Then the evening news hit me squarely in the pit of my stomach. The first feature dealt with the concern of pro-abortion women
that their clinics were being picketed by pro-life groups. "Harass-

27

ment" they called it, infringement upon a woman's right to make her own choice for her body. The soft-spoken, well-dressed chairperson reminded us that over one million women had chosen abortions in the past year and no amount of harassment would take away that right to choose.

The very next news item featured the opening of the Dallas Jewish Memorial to Holocaust Victims. One man whose seamed, care-worn face spoke volumes stated its purpose. "We must keep ever before us and never let us forget what man is capable of doing to man."

My mind silently screamed: But that is what mothers are doing right now to their own babies! Newspeople, don't you see what you have just shown? Can't you hear what you have just said? Why is one tragedy considered horrible while the other is acceptable? Why is pushing people into gas chambers more terrifying than pulling them out of mother's womb, which should be the safest place in all God's creation? Can't you understand that in a few short years the devastation of lives by means of abortion has surpassed the butchery of Hitler's Nazis? *Why can you not see that?*

The reason they cannot see the truth is simple. The value system of today's world is skewed away from truth. When values are not based upon Jesus Christ who is Truth and Life, then every-thing—including life itself—becomes relative to what is expedient for the moment. Once God's truth has been declared null and void there is no absolute ground left to stand on. Morality then changes with the shifting tides of public opinion. In our society today, God's Ten Commandments have been relegated to a mere ten suggestions. By and large, they are completely ignored, considered irrelevant to modern humanistic values.

GUARDING OUR MINDS

When the Lord tells us "to be sober," (Titus 2:4 KJV) He means for us to be clearheaded and disciplined. We must be able to think clearly in this most tumultuous of times. When every kind of group imaginable is screaming for its rights, we must know what God says is righteous. When public opinion says we are not "politically correct," we must continue to stand firmly for that which we know to be right, the eternal truth of God proclaimed in His Word. "The man without the Spirit does not accept the things that come from the Spirit of God, for they are foolishness to him, and he cannot understand them, because they are spiritually discerned . . . But we have the mind of Christ." (I Corinthians 2:14,16)

What a marvelous promise! We can have the mind of Christ. Satan is always battling for our minds. If he can upset our minds and emotions, he can keep us spinning off balance all the time. We must be watchful. We must guard our minds, our wills, our emotions, for this is the realm of the soul.

GUARDING OUR EMOTIONS

Women are emotional beings, sensitive, intuitive. God made us that way, so it is good. However, we must take care not to allow the enemy of our soul to prey upon our emotions. We are warned, "Gird up the loins of your mind." (I Peter 1:13 KJV) Do not give entrance to just any thing. For instance, if you absorb the kind of immorality portrayed daily on popular soap operas, you will gradually become desensitized to sin. Television holds insidious sway over modern morality. Be sober, be clearheaded about its power to color your own thinking.

How about radio? If you listen to the kinds of whining country and western songs whose express intent is to evoke sympathy for cheating lovers, you will find it easier to rationalize away God's absolute truth of marital fidelity. Much of today's rock music entices the listener into every sort of sexual encounter.

One by one our national moral standards have fallen, pushed over by popular demand. Divorce, homosexuality, adultery, transvestitism, abortion—all once rejected as sinful and degrading are now embraced and even promoted by a godless society.

The one sexual taboo left in our land is incest. No doubt in the coming days the media will begin to desensitize us in this area also, just as we have already become callous to homosexuality, adultery, murder, everything which once repelled us. The more we see degrading things portrayed in an acceptable, sympathetic storyline, the less sensitive we become, the less we recoil from their wickedness.

As I watch and weigh television programs, talk shows and movies, casual sex is everywhere present. Murder is explicitly real. Homosexuals are invariably shown to be kind and caring, while clergymen are portrayed as hypocrites. Magazines give point by point instructions on how to cast witchcraft spells. How to get your own way. How to win the man you want, even if he is another woman's husband. Manipulation is the name of today's game.

Some may argue that bringing such subjects into the open is healthy, for only then will people be able to talk about them and ultimately deal with them. If this is really the intent of the writers and producers, then why is the perpetrator of incest or adultery or abortion generally cast in a sympathetic light? Just watch, and you will see what I mean.

Be sober. Be clearheaded. Be disciplined. The Word warns, "The mind of sinful man is death, but the mind controlled by the Spirit is life and peace." (Romans 8:6) I have not mentioned these things to shock you. Indeed, we are probably past the point of being shocked by almost anything now. But we must be alert to see the kind of world which our children will think is normal, for they have known no other. They never knew the good old days of innocence before MTV and obscenity in public art museums. Before AIDS. Before Madonna.

IN THIS WORLD, NOT OF THIS WORLD

We must come to see ourselves as being *in* this world, but certainly not *of* this world. Jesus Himself prayed for us that we may be kept pure from the defilement around us: "My prayer is not that you take them out of the world but that you protect them from the evil one. They are not of the world, even as I am not of it." (John 17:15,16) You and I belong to a different kingdom, the Kingdom of God. However, we must be aware of what is happening all around us since it daily bombards us. We need not fear its impact as long as we are walking close to Jesus. He gives us this wonderful promise, "The peace of God, which transcends all understanding, will guard your hearts and your minds in Christ Jesus." (Philippians 4:7) Our hearts and minds are in His keeping. To be sure they remain there in that safe place, we are given very clear guidelines as to what we allow entrance into our hearts and minds: only those things which are true, noble, right, pure, lovely, admirable, excellent, and praiseworthy. (See Philippians 4:8)

By keeping our minds centered on positive, uplifting thoughts, we can much more easily communicate hope to those around us. We women set the emotional tone of our homes. We can minister courage to a world-weary husband who comes dragging his feet over the threshold at night. We can boost the confidence of a child who has that day failed a test or struck out at bat. We can offer comfort to that neighborhood teenager whose family is splintering. We can listen sympathetically to our friend who needs to let off steam before she explodes. We should make our home a haven of peace, comfort, and rest.

A PEACEFUL PLACE

Robert and I often laugh about whether or not to invite people into our home, because they never want to leave! It is not that we entertain them lavishly, not at all. People today are yearning for a peaceful place, and they find it in our home. Our sofa is comfortable and inviting. The tea kettle is always at the ready. Classical music quietly soothes. Soft colors and good art please the eye. Gentle manners call forth the best from visitors. And most important of all, the

31

presence of the Prince of Peace is there.

Recently a beautiful teenager opened her heart to me. "Do you know why I come to your house so much?" she asked. "It's because I find a real home and a real family here." This precious girl has been batted back and forth between her divorced mother and father all her life. She continued, "You sit down at the table together to eat your meals. We never do that at my house. We just grab something on the run—a sandwich, a pizza, whatever. You speak to each other quietly and kindly. At my house somebody is always yelling or griping. There is so much tension! I hope you don't mind if I just come sit here a while." Of course I assured her that she is welcome. How else can she learn to create her own peaceful place unless she sees a pattern to follow?

A PLACE OF SHELTER

Several years ago I was counseling a young woman whose jumpy nerves and gnawed fingernails betrayed a deep family problem. Throughout the session, our conversation seemed to wander, always avoiding what I suspected to be a serious emotional injury. Gently I asked questions. Cautiously, she offered guarded answers.

Finally, the conversation turned a corner, and she decided to to trust me. With tears, almost trembling, she told me the story. My heart broke as she shared the fearful events that would cause her to distrust, and even fear her own father.

For this young lady, home was anything but a place of safety and rest. She harbored a spirit of fearfulness that haunted every day of her life. It was the day-to-day presence of this fear that eventually pushed her to the edge of a breakdown. She was teetering there on the brink when I gently reached out a hand to pull her back. She sobbed, "I just can't go home right now. I just can't. Don't make me, please, don't make me go back." I scooped the child up in my arms, loved her, and rocked her like a baby. Then I called her mother and suggested it would be best for her to stay with me a few days. There was no response on the other end of the line. Her silence acquiescence confirmed the mother's awareness of the situation.

How thankful I was that I had a peaceful home in which she could rest. That exhausted child slept almost an entire week! Daily I could see the tension relax in her face. Robert and Kip and I loved on her, making her part of our family while she was there. The time of peace kept her from shattering.

KEEPING THE CUP FULL

How important, how urgent it is for us keepers at home to keep our lovingcup filled to the brim. You never know when your encouragement will change the course of a life. Have you listened with a lump in your throat as a hefty athlete gave the credit for his success to a mother who kept on inspiring him? Have you read through misty eyes the story of a foster mother who brought frightened, abused children into a new reality, a world where they could love and trust adults again? These are real people, like you and me, who keep on loving, caring, giving even in the face of seemingly insurmountable odds.

My mother was just such an encourager. She taught me from Day One, "Sissy, you can do *all* things through Jesus Christ who will give you the strength to accomplish what He calls you to do." (Philippians 4:13 is the source of her philosophy for living.) Whatever I really longed to do, I knew I could count on her support and prayers and help. My heart's desire was to go to college, even though it was financially impossible. Mother inspired me to work toward, believe for, and finally win the Alcoa Scholarship which completely funded my education.

When I knew God had put the dream in my heart to produce a Christian television program for children, I found nobody who believed I could do it—except Mother. The fulfilling day came when she made a guest appearance on "Backyard," my nationally syndicated children's program. Her eyes shone like stars, reflecting the bright lights on the set as she saw another dream come true. She had helped pray and encourage it into existence.

To be this kind of uplifter to our family and friends, we must allow the Lord time to encourage us, to fill up our cup. We need to maintain that positive mental attitude by meditating on His Word, His promises, and all the good blessings He continually brings. Too many times, however, we let down our guard. We allow the cares of this world to crowd in and cramp our minds. Unexpectedly, we find little or no spiritual energy to meet a sudden need. Instead of offering care and concern, we hear ourselves snapping, "Hey listen, I've had a rotten day too!"

THE EMOTIONAL WEATHERVANE

We all have bad days once in a while. I wish we didn't, but we do. Nothing knocks my family off kilter more quickly than when Mom has a Bad Day. If it is so bad that I am reduced to tears, my husband gets panicky and my son morose. Atmospheric gloom descends upon our usually happy home. All because I am the emotional weathervane in our house. Fortunately, my bad days are few and far between. When they do slip up on my blind side, I generally find one recurring reason: time pressure.

Time pressure is a phenomenon of modern life. We have so many time saving devices in our homes that we feel we have extra time to get involved in causes, classes, or crises. One good idea leads to another. Before long we are inextricably bound up with more obligations than we can handle. Pressure mounts. Time pressure which brings tension, banishes peace, and besets our quiet time with the Lord.

If you are a doer, an achiever, the temptation to overload yourself with responsibilities is one against which you must stand guard. A continual overload will eventually lead to burnt-out circuits. I had to learn this most difficult lesson the hard way. Here is how it happened:

I was rushing around that bright autumn afternoon, trying as usual to accomplish too many things in too little time. One of my many stops was to pick up some labels at the printshop for Mother. Since Daddy was retired and Mother loved to bake, they had decided to open "Eva's Pie Shoppe." The whole family was cheering them on. My contribution to the cause, because I knew printing, was to have professional-looking labels made for the pie boxes.

My dismayed shriek rose above the clattering presses when I examined the work. Every bright green and white label proudly proclaimed the *wrong* telephone number! What a stupid error this printer had made. Biting back my anger, I declared he would have to do the whole job over. Patiently the mild man pulled out my original artwork. I was stunned! I saw the two wrong digits written by my own hand. The man had printed exactly what I gave him. My tears welled up and spilled over as I turned to go.

"Hey, little lady," the printer tried to comfort me, "no need to cry. We all make mistakes. Let's just do it over and get it right this time." I simply shook my head, groped for the door, and blindly stumbled out into the sunshine, leaving a puzzled man staring after me, wondering why I took it so hard.

What frightened me was not the wasted time or money for the labels. It was the fact that these kinds of mistakes were occurring with increased frequency in my fast-paced life. Always an organizer who could get things together, I was seeing them fall apart again and again. Simple mistakes. Forgetting things. Thinking I had done one thing only to find I had done something entirely different, such as this printing error. What was happening to my mind? It was scary.

RIDING OFF IN ALL DIRECTIONS

The main person God has given to help me see clearly is my husband Robert. I poured out my frustrations and fears to him. Then he put his finger square dab on the problem. Husbands have an uncanny way of doing that because God has given them the charge to care for us. "Honey, I believe the Lord has fired a warning shot over the bow of your little ship because He wants you to change course," Robert said. "You are riding off in all directions trying to accomplish too many things at once. God wants you to slow down and learn to rest in Him. You don't have to do anything *for* Him. Just let Him do what He wants to do *through* you."

Robert spoke the truth. At that particular time I was attempting to fill all these positions: wife, mother, pastor's wife, church musician, television producer, fundraiser, PTA president, Community Library Board member, Sunday School teacher, women's group leader, and drama coach to the Wildwood Players. I was constantly rushing from one deadline to the next. I rarely took time to listen to the still, small Voice calling, "Be still and know that I am God." (Psalm 46:10) My rushing around in a whirl of good activities precluded that most important time of all, time alone with the Restorer of my soul. For that reason my emotions were ragged, my temper frayed, my energy spent.

All these were good activities, I hasten to add. Nothing was wrong with any of them. I enjoyed them all. There were simply too many.

Imagine carrying a stack of books. Good books, interesting books, even Christian books which edify and encourage. You pick up the first two, then add this one, yes, and that study guide too. Before you realize it, you are staggering under a load of eight books. When someone dumps a couple of heavy ones on top (as always happens when you least expect it) suddenly you are overloaded. You simply cannot carry them all at once. We pick up our activities like this, one at a time. Mostly they are worthwhile and enjoyable. Often they bring us esteem in the eyes of others, which is rewarding.

"Oh, you are so creative! Always coming up with the best ideas for our group of ladies."

"Here is the President's Cup of Service for our Volunteer of the Year."

"You must be the world's best organizer, the way you put that Spring Festival together for our PTA. It was the most successful event ever!"

You smile graciously, all the while wishing you could go sit beside a bubbling brook and listen to a mockingbird sing.

OUT OF THE TANGLED STRINGS

I am grateful that God stopped me in my tracks and caused me to reexamine my priorities. Step by step He helped me extricate myself from the tangled strings of false responsibility I had wound around myself and my family. He used my quiet time to show me clearly the vital issues of my life: my relationship with Him, with Robert, with my son, with my extended family. Would it matter that I had a national television ministry if I allowed it to consume so much of me that my personal life fell apart? Who would care whether or not my name was on the Founders Plaque in the Community Library ten years from now? Which was more important, having time to picnic with my son and answer his questions or spending countless hours on the telephone with committees? Of what value was it to be known as a real go-getter in the community if my own husband could not find me when he needed me?

These were hard questions for me at that time. But it is exactly these kinds of "bottom line" answers we must find as wives and mothers. Get alone with the Lord. Let Him set your priorities. Then stick to them.

FINDING A SENSE OF QUIET

Many years ago Anne Morrow Lindbergh spoke lucidly to this need of ours in her gem of a book, "Gift from the Sea." From her chapter on the Moon Shell:

"Woman's life today is tending more and more toward the state William James describes so well in the German word, 'Zerrissenheit—torn-to-pieces-hood.' She cannot live perpetually in 'Zerrissenheit.' She will be shattered into a thousand pieces. On the contrary, she must consciously encourage those pursuits which oppose the centrifugal forces of today. Quiet time alone, contemplation, prayer, music, a centering line of thought or reading, of study or work. It can be physical or intellectual or artistic, any creative life proceeding from oneself. It need not be an enormous project or a great work. But it should be something of one's own. Arranging a bowl of flowers in the morning can give a sense of quiet in a crowded day—like writing a poem, or saying a prayer. What matters is that one be for a time inwardly attentive." (p. 50, Random House)

She goes on to ponder why women today have been seduced into abandoning this inner strength in order to prove ourselves equal to men. Why indeed?

The Lord God Himself gave us the key to wholeness when He promised, "In quietness and trust is your strength." (Isaiah 30:15) Then He observed, "But you would have none of it."

We must establish priority times of quietness to be with the Lord in order to regain our confidence. Waiting upon Him renews our strength. (See Isaiah 40:31) Even Jesus Himself drew apart from all the excitement of ministry and miracles to restore His soul by being with the Father. If He needed times like this, how much more do we?

TAKE TIME ALONE

Tell your family that in order to be the kind of wife and mother they need, you must have an inviolate time alone with the Lord. It may be early in the morning or during the children's afternoon nap or after the household settles down at night. It may be only fifteen minutes, but it must be consistent.

Now and then try to find time to go on a prayer retreat. I

prefer to go alone. You may like to go with a group of ladies. When I am feeling emotionally frayed, I know it is time for me to head for the hills where the Lord has provided a quiet place for me. My husband very graciously takes charge of the household for a couple of days. Obviously this is a season of my life when it is easier for me to take alone time than when our son Kipling was small and dependent.

I highly value these special times when I leave the hustle and bustle of people, places, and pressures in the city to have time with the Restorer of my soul. On one such occasion this poem flowed out from me. I call it "Time":

> Time to be
> Simply me.
> No responsibility.
>
> Time to pray.
> Time to say,
> "Lord, just You and me today."
>
> Time to rest.
> Time to test
> All things and hold fast the best.
>
> Time to fast.
> Leave the past.
> Body comes in line at last.
>
> Time to mend
> Thoughts that rend.
> Cleanse the broken heart that sinned.
>
> Time to heal.
> Time to kneel
> To heed the Voice so soft and still.

You will have to make room for your quiet time. It will not just happen. The enemy of your soul will see to that, for he does not want you to be renewed in confidence and strength. He likes to see you harried and hassled and hurt. Do not let him intrude into your special time with the Lord, as you may be sure he will try to do.

A THOUSAND DISTRACTIONS

For instance, sometimes we set apart a space of time when we say, "Lord, this quiet time is just for You and me." We begin to read the Word or try to pray when, lo and behold, we realize our minds are completely elsewhere. We are hearing again that little zinger of a comment Marie directed at us. Or we recall that striking red dress at the mall which we almost bought, and still might if we can figure it into our budget. Or we worry about the stress that seems to be intensifying at our husband's office. Or any of a thousand other diversionary thoughts. Then the telephone rings, the children wake up from their naps, it is time to start dinner, and today's quiet time with the Lord is ended before it has begun.

Did you know that you can command your soul to come in line with your spirit? Remember, your soul is the area of your mind, will, and emotions. Your spirit longs to spend time with its Restorer, but the soul often gets in the way. When that happens, simply speak Psalm 116:7 to yourself, "Return unto thy rest, O my soul." In other words, "Be still, emotions. Be quiet, mind. Listen, will." Why? "For the Lord hath dealt bountifully with thee." (KJV)

KEEPING THE WORD ALIVE WITHIN US

The Book of Psalms contains a whole banquet of choice food for your emotional self. We should all commit to memory as many of these wonderful verses as we can. Then they are always with us, to

40

aid, to comfort, to reassure, to bring peace to troubled emotions.

One day my dear friend Jerry Rose learned the value of scripture memory in a most poignant way. Jerry's days were filled with stress, for he managed a busy television station. This specific day as he stood in his office, Jerry began to feel quite peculiar. He suddenly realized that he could not tell time, could not think of his name, could not even call for help. Jerry was suffering a stress-related seizure. Thank God that his secretary heard him as he fell onto his desk, then toppled to the floor. While the ambulance raced toward the hospital with attendants attaching life-sustaining equipment to his body, Jerry realized his mind had fixed on one anchor: "Yea, though I walk through the valley of the shadow of death, I shall fear no evil, for thou art with me." His mind knew he was in that awful valley of the shadow, so his spirit called upon the secure rock of comfort he had known since childhood, Psalm 23. Jerry clung tenaciously to its promise, "I shall fear no evil, no evil, no evil—for thou art with me, you are here, you are with me." His spirit had confidence that the Great Physician was right there in the emergency room. His Shepherd was guiding him through that dark valley. Jerry came through the ordeal with no lingering physical effects, but with the victorious knowledge that God's Word is indeed alive for us.

HIS WORD OUR DEFENSE, OUR VICTORY

Once when our family had been fighting a particularly difficult time of spiritual warfare, we drove home to find a witch's hex painted on the street in front of our house. Fear, the devil's mighty weapon, came hurtling straight at me. But the Lord has promised that when the enemy comes in like a flood, the Spirit of God will raise up His standard against it. (Isaiah 59:19 KJV) The standard He raised in my behalf this time was Psalm 91. Immediately I recalled, "There shall no evil befall thee, neither shall any plague come nigh thy dwelling. For he shall give his angels charge over thee, to keep thee in all thy ways." (vs. 10,11 KJV) Poof! Fear dissolved. I went out and stomped on the crude drawing (See Genesis 3:15) while my son painted a cross right over the top of it and my husband proclaimed Jesus to be Lord of that whole street!

I am so grateful for the comforting, uplifting Psalms!

One unhappy time I was belittled unjustly before a group of my peers. I was not given the opportunity to speak in my own behalf. How it stung! Holding my emotions in check until I could seek the solace of my own room, I flung myself across my bed and wept bitterly into the cushiony coverlet. "God, why, why, why?" I questioned. "It's not fair!" He waited until the tempest of emotion had passed, but before thoughts of revenge came slithering up. He led me into Psalm 119. Right there in verse 165 He spoke clearly to my situation: "Great peace have they which love thy law, and nothing shall offend them." (KJV) Nothing. Nothing. Nothing shall offend them! That verse settled into my spirit, from whence it has been called upon more than a few times.

Psalms of praise lift you up when you are down. Sing psalms of joy to bless the Lord and edify your spirit. Let God speak to you through these life-giving words that have ministered to saints through ages past. They are anointed and encouraging.

THE EQUAL TIME LAW

A dear old godly pastor, Sam Eldridge, always managed to keep a clear perspective and level head in the midst of every crisis. One day I asked him the secret of his consistent, calm spirit. Uncle Sam smiled his sweet, slow smile and replied, "It's easy when you observe the Equal Time Law."

The Equal Time Law? What in the world?

"JoAn, you have been involved in media. You know that when someone offers a controversial point of view the television station must offer equal time to the opposing viewpoint. For example, the Democrats always have time to respond to whatever the Republicans have just said. That is the Equal Time Law."

"Yes, but . . . how does it work in your own life, or mine?"

"Well, when the enemy brings worrisome thoughts or doubts into my mind, I simply give God equal time to bring His point of view across to me. Spend as much time praying about a situation as you spend worrying about it. It's amazing how quickly it all works out."

Uncle Sam was right. Many times since then when I found myself fretting over some situation, I just invoked the Equal Time Law. I would realize I had spent fifteen fruitless minutes worrying about something over which I had no control. So I would switch off those troubling thoughts by saying, "Lord, I now give You equal time. The next fifteen minutes are Yours. You're the One in control of this situation anyway." It is amazing how much calmer you are after fifteen minutes of prayer than the same time spent in worry.

Remember the Equal Time Law.

GUARDING OUR WORDS

One of the most vital areas of our lives where we must be constantly vigilant and clearheaded is the realm of communication with others. Everywhere we turn today we see advice offered on ways to close the communication gap.

Husband with wife.

Parents with teenagers.

Employer and employee.

Older people with their grown children.

Business with labor.

All this advice points up one important fact: People have lost the ability to speak their hearts. Few can deliver truth without giving offense. True communicators are few and far between. Gracious speaking has become a lost art.

God's Word is the original, authentic handbook on communication. The Book of Proverbs alone contains a wealth of sage counsel on the importance of our words. Think about this statement, "Death and life is in the power of the tongue." (Proverbs 18:21 KJV) We can shrivel people with our tongue or we can make them blossom. Blasting or blooming? We can call forth either response from those around us by the way we speak.

A common scene these days is a harried mother pushing her cart through the grocery aisles with a three-year-old tugging at her arm, urging her to buy this and buy that (all of which he saw on TV). Finally Mom turns on him in frustration with a scathing rejoinder, usually accompanied by a smack for emphasis. He wilts under the blast. His little face crumples. The wonder of his seeing the reality of those commercials is suddenly snuffed out by Mom's impatience. The shopping trip is no longer fun. He begins to whine, further taxing his poor mother's already short temper.

Have you seen a father lose patience with his son because the child simply can't get the hang of the game? Possibly due to his own embarrassment, Dad barks out a belittling description of his son's physical abilities. And the needle labeled "Inferiority" cuts a deeper groove in a shy little guy's waning self-confidence.

WORDS THAT LAST A LIFETIME

If these parents could see into their children's souls, if they could realize that the damage they are inflicting bit by bit will scar a whole lifetime, no doubt they would watch their words more carefully. Perhaps they would pray this vital prayer each day, "Set a guard over my mouth, O Lord: keep watch over the door of my lips." (Psalm 141:3)

Have you flung words at your husband to wish them instantly unsaid even as they hung on the air? Do you find yourself saying too often, "I'm so sorry, I didn't really mean to say that"?

Why *did* you say it? The old counting-to-ten-before-you-reply advice carries a great deal of wisdom. Words once said can be apologized over, but they can never, ever be unsaid. They will come back to haunt you when you least expect it. Therefore, be wise. "Keep your tongue from evil and your lips from speaking lies. Turn from evil, and do good; seek peace and pursue it." (Psalm 34:13,14) A pattern for us is the Proverbs 31 woman who "openeth her mouth with wisdom; and in her tongue is the law of kindness." (vs. 26 KJV)

CHANGING THE INGRAINED PATTERNS

Perhaps you have vowed again and again to stop sinning with your tongue. Have you failed to keep that vow? Ask the Lord to reveal why you have such a problem. If you were verbally abused as a child, you have strong patterns of behavior ingrained in your very thought-processes which only the cleansing blood of Jesus Christ can erase. If you have deep feelings of inferiority, you must ask the Lord to restore your soul. If you have an ungovernable temper and tend to speak your mind, you need deliverance from the stronghold that years of self-indulgence have built into your heart.

Any sin of the tongue can be forgiven and changed by the Lord Jesus Christ. Psalm 91:15 promises, "He will call upon me, and I will answer him; I will be with him in trouble, I will deliver him, and honor him." Truly God will be with us in times of trouble. He will deliver us out of the bondage of our past. We must be willing to be changed, to let Him make of us a new creation.

RESPONDING OR REACTING?

One of the most wonderful things about living for God is that He always picks us up when we fall, brushes us off, and gives us a new place to begin. Ask the Lord each day for help with your tongue, to begin to respond rather than react. Reactions happen instantly, without thought. When reacting to a situation, you are usually less than clearheaded. If you allow time to think the situation through, you will respond in a more Christlike way.

Did you know God wants to wear out your "reactor"? What causes your hackles to rise? That is quite likely the very thing the Holy Spirit wants to deal with in your life. Why do you become so defensive about a particular subject? You may have a gaping hole in your emotional being that the Lord wants to fill up with His grace. Does being near a certain person seem automatically to set a chip on your shoulder? Jesus is trying to teach you to love and forgive. He does not intend for you to carry around a load of hostilities and fears. He wants your shoulders "chip free"!

We must give God our right to react. We must allow Him to be our defense. We must turn loose of those old hurts. Until we do, we will find ourselves often in situations which challenge these areas and bring the opportunity to grow.

A HIGHWAY FOR HIS GLORY

In the early days of our traveling ministry, Robert and I had opportunity to peer behind the scenes of many different churches. I remember with amusement and some chagrin our introduction to one particular place. As the pastor guided us around the lovely facility he said, "We're really looking forward to this series of meetings. We expect to see the glory of the Lord." We delightedly concurred. Then he asked Robert, "By the way, does your wife play the piano?" Robert assured him that I did play and would be happy to teach some new worship songs to the congregation. "Oh, no, no," this pastor hastily declined. "Please don't play at all while you're here. You see, our pianist is very touchy. She thinks she *owns* that piano, and if anybody else touches it in the service, all hell will break loose around here!"

Slightly dazed, I declared that I would indeed stay clear of that piano. After all, we hoped all heaven would break loose. Realistically though, there was not much opportunity for such release of God's glory in that place. As my wise husband commented later, "If God has to bring in His glory by way of a crooked, bumpy road that twists around touchy pianists, wary pastors, and pew-hardened people, He would just rather not. I wish I could drive a spiritual bulldozer through this place, piano and all!"

We must purpose to allow our Master builder all the spiritual and emotional excavation, reformation, and transformation He chooses to do in us. Let's let Him build in our lives a highway for His glory to come rolling through.

PEACE IN THE TURMOIL

Another vital area in the realm of being sober is the ability to make clearheaded decisions in the midst of a crisis. As Rudyard Kipling said so beautifully in his poem "If",

If you can keep your head
When all about you men are losing theirs
And blaming it on you . . .
You'll be a man, my son.

As God's children, we must be able to discern the mind of Christ in any given situation and try to bring peace into the turmoil, order into the chaos. Crisis experiences test our inner mettle to the limit and let us see clearly how strong (or weak) we really are.

WORDS OF DEATH, WORDS OF LIFE

Once I was waiting quietly at church for our people to gather for prayer meeting. Robert was out of state on a speaking tour. Suddenly one of our teenagers burst through the door screaming, "Oh, it's horrible, Mrs. Summers! He's dying, he's dying!" I tried to calm her enough to give me a coherent statement. Linnie had just seen a motor-cycle wreck. The driver had not been wearing his helmet. His mangled body was pinned under the wreckage. Though panicky, Linnie retained enough presence of mind to realize that our church was just over the hill and we could bring help.

Dispatching someone to call an ambulance, I hurried out with her, hoping to render aid. When we arrived at the scene, we saw about 25 people already collected there, standing around in a circle giving wide berth to all the blood and gore. No one was helping the poor man. They were just gawking.

"Nawp, he ain't gonna make it. He's a goner, fer sure."

"Plumb stupid not to wear his helmet."

"Lookie there, he's started bleedin' at the mouth. Must have lots of internal injuries."

"Bleedin' from his ear too. That's brain damage. If he lives, he'll probably just be a vegetable."

Horrified, I listened to their brutal comments. They all had the power of life and death in their tongues, and they were condemning him to death. Desperately I prayed, "Oh, God, stop their mouths! How can I minister life to this poor, wounded man?"

The answer came, immediate and crystal clear to my inner being: *Get on your knees and pray for him.*

"You mean, right here – in front of everybody? Right now?"

Here and now.

I chose to obey. Right there on the blood-splattered highway I knelt down beside the limp body, placed my hand on his back, and began to pray.

Everybody froze. Silence fell. It was amazing! Like praying in a hushed cathedral. Not a soul uttered another word as they stood around watching this strange lady beseech God for a man's life to be spared.

Finally I could make out the distant wail of the ambulance. Leaning close to the man's ear I spoke clearly, "Hold on, help is almost here. Don't give up. God is with you. I have prayed for you and you're going to be alright. Do you understand me?"

From the depths of his being, he managed a groan and slight nod. This man was conscious! He had heard all those dreadful predictions about his future. But he had also received the words of life and hope being ministered to him.

The paramedics carefully bundled him up, and the vehicle screamed away toward our local hospital. The crowd shook off its spell of astonishment. Different folk began recounting other tales of wounding and woe as they dispersed. We returned to our prayer meeting to pray that God's healing power would restore the poor victim to wholeness and new life.

That is not the end of the story. God gave me an unexpected thrill of pleasure when, only four days later, I saw that man at the County Fair. Oh yes, he was all scraped and cut and bruised, hobbling around on crutches, but he was very much alive! I just smiled and nodded as we passed each other. He will never know who that lady was who prayed for him, but he can never doubt that God loved him enough to send her in his moment of desperate need.

GUARDING THE WELLSPRING

Strength in crisis. Grace under pressure. Emotionally together. Truth over illusion. Wise mouths, kind tongues.

These are all part of being sober. We must guard our hearts from the insistent hammering of the world around us. "Above all else, guard your heart, for it is the wellspring of life." (Proverbs 4:23)

As our beloved pastor Des Evans summed up in his inimitable Welsh way, "If the whole world is shouting Yea! but the Lord God frowns a No, then the answer is No. However, if the crowds are booing and the whole world seems against you, yet the Lord says Hurrah! — then Hurrah, indeed it is!"

CHAPTER 3

TO HAVE AND TO HOLD

"to love their husbands"
Titus 2:4

W eddings are wonderful, I thrilled, watching our dear Rod at the altar with his bride. What makes every wedding so special, so unique?

It is more than the beautiful bride arrayed in purity and white, shimmering in the light of love. More than the soft glow of candles and fragrance of the bridal bouquet. More than the caresses of the string quartet's lovesongs. The wonder comes with that holy hush descending as we hear the sacred vows solemnly declared before God:

"to have and to hold,
to love and to cherish,
from this day forward,
so long as we both shall live."

We see that covenant sealed with a kiss of promise, and suddenly there is a miracle standing before us! Right before our eyes two people have bonded their lives into one, beginning a whole new family unit. No wonder we thrill to the sight of it. No wonder we rejoice when the pastor turns them to us and proudly presents "Mr. and Mrs. Roderick Paul Butler."

What a special, triumphant time!

Rod is our spiritual son. He came to us first as a vital part of our television ministry. Later he came to be a vital part of our family. Living with us for two years, Rod became the big brother our son Kip had always longed for. As the years passed by, Rod began to look for that "other half" of himself, the lifelong partner he needed. In our family he watched the ups and downs of marriage in everyday life. Giving, taking. Fuming, forgiving. Loving, living. Exciting highs, stressful lows. Rod saw it all.

Finally he was ready to put his learning into living. He moved to another city to join the ministry team of a large, dynamic church. Within a few months he met the love of his life. And to top it all off, he said, "Jeri has a wonderful big family that I can just snuggle into like a glove—aunts, uncles, cousins, and all!"

Now here they stand before us, gallantly facing the future together as husband and wife. For a brief moment Rod catches my eye and flashes a broad grin that says, "My miracle happened. Here we are at last!"

WEATHERING ANY STORM

As they serve the Lord together in ministry, they have the sweet assurance that their marriage will last a lifetime. There will be good times and bad ones, a few rocks and shocks along the way, blending with years of blessing and contentment. How can I say this so surely? Cynics will scoff, pointing to today's high divorce rate. But my certainty abides in the knowledge that Rod and Jeri are building their lives together on the Rock, Christ Jesus. On such a foundation, they can weather any storm life hurls at them.

Today it is tragic to see so many couples set sail together on the sea of love only to find their high hopes shattering into salty tears.

In bits and pieces the wreckage of lives floats off in many directions, scattering what God had intended as an ark of safety, the family. The refugees from that storm huddle together, forming new family units, trying harder to weather adverse gales the second time around.

A GLIMMER OF HOPE

With all the media attention on today's divorce rate, remarriage statistics, stepparenting, blended families, and the so-called demise of the nuclear family, it is easy to lose sight of the fact that *most marriages do hold together*. Although it is not easy to withstand the assaults on today's family structure, still the unit established by God in the very beginning is not about to perish from the face of this earth.

I believe we are beginning to see a turn in our society, a poignant yearning for stability. We hear songs which long for love to last, for family ties to endure. Such as the Judds' nostalgic tune "Grandpa, tell me about the good old days."

Popular art reflects popular thought. So it is very heartening to see an upsurge in television programs and movies and magazine reports about family values. By no means is the amount of coverage equal that given to immorality and destructive values. As one friend said, "Most entertainment today is half and half: half corn and half porn." But there is a glimmer of hope.

Surely everyone in our nation recognizes that the fabric which weaves us together as a civilized society, our family, is being ripped to shreds. The first step to solving a problem is the recognition that it indeed exists and demands a solution. Experts cannot agree on the root of this problem. Therefore, they cannot find a scientific cure to dispense. Some say the divorce rate is caused by all the stress of modern society. Others say our culture is evolving into a new phase in which the traditional family will be passe. Still others cite the fact that today's career/wife and career/husband have no role models to pattern their career-oriented life after, and so end their marriages after too many trial and error mistakes. The theories go on and on. But the experts are not squarely facing the problem in the light of absolute truth.

COVENANT BREAKERS

PROBLEM: Why are marriages shattering into divorce at an unprecedented rate?

ANSWER: People have become covenant breakers.

What??

Covenant breakers. People no longer keep their vows. They are no longer "as good as their word." How many business deals today close on a simple handshake? No way! They are bound up as right and tight as fourteen Philadelphia lawyers can make them, then signed in triplicate.

This faithlessness (which has caused the legal profession to flourish beyond belief in our time) has insinuated its slimy deception into the sanctity of the home.

SOLUTION: Recognize a covenant for what it is—an eternal vow before Almighty God. Honor it as such. Otherwise, do not enter into it.

A LIFETIME COMMITMENT

When Robert and I counsel young people planning marriage, we have them firmly and carefully consider the wedding covenant. This is serious business, not to be taken lightly because they are giddy from the effects of stardust and moonbeams and rainbows. To be sure, love and romance are vital elements. But this commitment must last *forever*, even when the time comes, as it does to every romance, that the luster is no longer bright. These two people need to pray earnestly over their decision, be sure they have peace with the Lord about it, weigh it carefully, and settle it in their hearts for all time. Only then should they stand before God to declare their vows, covenanting with one another, "Until death do us part."

Once we have taken that vow, there is no backing out. No "whoops, it's not as fun as I thought it was gonna be." Nor, "I just don't love him like I thought I did." Think about what you have pledged before God to do with this man: "to have and to hold, to love and to cherish, for better or for worse, in sickness and in health, forsaking all others, cleave only to him so long as we both shall live." That is a definite lifetime commitment. Small wonder that many couples today are choosing to write their own vows rather than honoring the traditional promise.

When that man of God who pronounces you man and wife solemnly intones, "What God hath joined together, let no man put asunder," he is not just saying some flowery marital Amen. Rather, he is sealing this marriage ceremony with the very words of Jesus Himself. When Christ was questioned about divorce in Matthew 19, He replied that husband and wife were no longer two separate people, "but one flesh. What therefore God hath joined together, let not man put asunder." (vs. 6 KJV) Even in Jesus' day people were looking for ways to renege on their marriage covenant. In the two thousand years since, this problem has only compounded.

However, God's attitude toward covenant breakers remains unchanged. God hates people who break covenant. In fact, He places them in the same category with murderers and other wicked evildoers. You can read this plainly in Romans 1:29 -32.

EQUAL, LOVING PARTNERS

God Himself established marriage for the very first man and woman. When He saw that it was not good for man to be alone, He created a helpmate for Adam. (See Genesis 2.) Is it not fascinating how God fashioned this special woman? He could have scooped up more dirt. Instead, He made a refinement of man. Causing a deep sleep to come over Adam, divine anesthesia if you will, God extracted a rib from Adam's side to use as the source material for this woman, Eve. What a remarkable bone for God to choose. Not one from the foot, that man would keep her underfoot and subjected. Nor a bone from the head, that woman might try to rule over man and be his superior. Rather, God chose a rib.

Consider the rib's position: right next to the heart so that she might ever be close to his heart, and just under his arm so that he might hold her close for protection and nurturing. Side by side they stand, equal, loving partners. Forever joined, as Adam declared when he drew Eve into his arms, "This is now bone of my bones, and flesh of my flesh."

BRINGING OUT THE BEST

Just as Eve was the refinement of her husband, God intends for you to be the refinement of that lifetime partner you have chosen. God has placed within you an innate quality which can bring out the very best in your man. To you is given the ability to inspire him to the heights of being his best. How do you do this? With love and honor, encouragement and much prayer for him. When you *know* he can do it, accomplish it, change it, your man will go to almost any length to justify your faith in him.

I have seen far more wives than I care to count doing exactly the opposite. Instead of encouraging, they nag. Rather than pray, they push. Bit by bit their critical spirit dooms their man to failure or alienation.

WARNING: The male ego is rather fragile, easily crushed by the one he loves. Handle with prayer.

Since the dawn of civilization when God joined Adam and Eve in what surely was the most beautiful garden wedding of all time, every wedding has been sacred to Him. No doubt He watches from the portals of Heaven as two people covenant with each other "in the sight of God" to join their lives together from now on.

NO MATTER WHAT HAPPENS

An absolute, bedrock principle for beginning your lives together is that once you are committed to marriage you stay with it no matter what happens. Yes, there will be problems and even some heartbreak. But stay with it.

When you honor your vows, you are honoring God. Please know that He can work out all the problems. Lay down your pride. Be a strong woman of God. Make it work. Remember, you have help. The power of the Holy Spirit within will equip you to keep the love of your husband all your life long. Please do not give up when the going gets rough. If you hold on, you can make it.

When my wonderful friends John and Jan married, they were a most unlikely pair. She came from a loving, vocal, outgoing, closeknit family. John's family was quiet, withdrawn, never showing affection. John once remarked that he had never in his life seen his father hug his mother. Coming from such opposite family patterns, these two young people had quite a crash course in blending their lifestyles. In fact, there were times when it seemed to verge on all-out war. Compounding the problem was the fact that Jan worked full-time to support John while he finished college. It was difficult for her to defer to his decisions while she was earning the income. There were tearful, bitter times, then painful adjustments for both of them, followed by growing maturity.

The foreverness of this couple did not just happen. They had to make it work. There were times when we trembled for their future. But Jan never gave up! Even when her own family doctor counseled divorce to get her out of such a stressful life, she never wavered. She and John were in that marriage for the duration. They had made their vows before God!

59

THE DIVINE ERASER

Yes, the Lord was faithful. Through many dangers, toils, and snares, He led them by His amazing grace. His mercy upheld them. Today they are truly one flesh, pastoring a great church, capable counselors of God's love, parents of two fine sons. Robert and I were surprise guests at their 25th wedding anniversary celebration. They are still obviously in love with one another.

Once I asked Jan if the enemy ever used those bitter memories of the past against John. She just smiled and shook her head. "Jo, I know we had terrible battles back then, but God has been so gracious to remove every trace of emotional pain connected with that period of our lives. I can't even call it into focus. It's just a distant, hazy memory."

That is the wonderful grace of Jesus! His divine eraser totally removed every harsh word and painful scene. He brought true, lasting forgiveness. Those hurts are forgiven *and* forgotten, buried in the sea of forgetfulness. Truly the mercies of the Lord are "new every morning." (See Lamentations 3:22,23.) Each new day we can claim the mercy of God to renew our hearts and minds, to restore our marriage, to return us to the time of our first love.

NURTURING THE FIRST LOVE

It is essential that we keep an essence of the first love we enjoyed with our husbands. Think back to those beginning days of bridal bliss. Didn't your beloved come first with you in everything? If he liked shortie pajamas on you while you preferred flannel grannygowns, weren't all the grannies banished? If he liked cherry cheesecake best of all, what did you surprise him with on your first month's anniversary? (With a little help from Sara Lee.) If he wanted to have the guys over to watch the big game, didn't you pop the corn and make the snacks and show them all what a truly choice pick of a wife their buddy had made? Of course you did. I did too.

My point is that you wanted to please him in every way. He was first priority in your life. That is how it should be. Your relationship to your husband comes second only to your commitment to God. Have your priorities shifted? Are you putting other things, other people before this primary relationship?

It is unrealistic to think you will always have that emotional high, that first thrill of discovery which makes the bridal chamber so special. Emotions do mellow out over the years into a deep, abiding love. Even though the initial giddiness may be gone when you have been married twenty years, you do still need some giddy times. Make it a priority to have times alone together, just the two of you, when you flirt and tease and romance one another. Bring back the glamour into your marriage. Bring back your first love.

THE SUBTLE SNARE

This is hard to accomplish when you are tired and fat and worried. Somehow you have let everyone and everything else push in ahead of him to demand your care and attention. Too many wives do this—unwittingly at first. They take for granted that dear old faithful husband will always be there. Other things gradually creep in to divert their attention. Their priorities get switched. They may not even be aware of it. However, dear old faithful husband is acutely aware of it. He is being set up slowly but surely for the enemy's subtle snare.

When a husband realizes he no longer holds first place in his wife's heart, he becomes terribly vulnerable. The enemy of home and fidelity is Satan, who continually prowls around seeking prey to devour. (I Peter 5:8) A hurting husband is easy game for him. Satan simply brings another woman into his path to tempt him, to tell him how wonderful he is, to flatter and finally seduce him. The line usually goes something like this: "Your wife just doesn't know how to appreciate you. Sigh. If I had a man like you . . ." Wham! The trap springs. The marriage shatters. The devil chortles.

FIRST, FOREMOST, AND FOREVER

Wives, we must love our husbands, first, foremost and forever. Keep telling them. Keep showing them. Keep tucking little
lovenotes into their briefcases or lunchboxes. Your man needs your
reassurance. A man who can go out and daily butt heads in the frantic
marketplace is not tough at all when it comes to the love of his life.

I believe this one single issue of taking one another for granted,
this lack of appreciation is at the root of divorces where the couple has
been married twenty to thirty years. To leave a partner in whom you
have invested thirty years of your life is inconceivable to me. What
does that mean? What does your life count for if you spend thirty
years of it with someone, then decide you made a mistake? Mid-life
madness! Just when you reach the point where the children are launched
and you finally have time to be alone, to recapture romance?

Ah, but that's the problem. The romance must continue all
through the family's growing years. Otherwise, when the children are
gone you may suddenly look at one another and think, "Who are you?"
Never allow yourselves to become strangers merely sleeping in the
same bed. Keep the priority of one another first.

WHEN TWO BECOME THREE

When does it enter a marriage, this tendency to shift priorities? Not as a new bride, of course. We have already remembered that
you wanted to please him in every way then. So let's look at the next
stage: the marvelous birth of that first baby. It brings so many changes.
Two become one, and now they have become three.

A very good trend in childbirth is developing, that of allowing
the husband to be part of the birthing process. No longer is he shoved
off into a smoke-filled waiting room to pace and worry. Now he can
be right by his wife's side, coaching her, loving her, timing her. He
can be there to cheer when the tiny one finally peeps out at the bright

lights of the birthing theater. He can count the ten fingers and toes, marvel how much hair his baby already has. He becomes part of the wonder. He knows firsthand the reality of "this life we have brought into the world."

Bringing a new baby home, particularly the first child, drastically alters a couple's lifestyle. Wife, make the effort to include your husband in as many loving ways as you can. Be sure it does not become a "baby and me doing our thing together" while husband feels shamed by the first twinge of jealousy over being left out. Always remember this is *our* baby, *our* precious one. Do not allow your priority to begin shifting at this most special time of your marriage. Creating new life together should draw you two even closer, not drive a wedge of separation.

One helpful hint: Try to regain your shapely figure as soon as possible. Of necessity your sex life has been curtailed during the last stages of pregnancy. Most men can be lovingly patient only so long. Make it your goal to slim down quickly and be sexually appealing again. He will appreciate you for trying, for wanting to please him, for showing that he is still at the top of your priority list.

PUSHED IN TO THE BACKGROUND

As the family becomes established and the children start to school, wife usually gets involved with new activities. This is especially true if the children are successful and popular. She may get all wrapped up in what they are doing, reliving her youth through them. On the other hand, if the children have problems, she may become consumed with tutors and helpers and homework. Subtly, things happen to push husband into the background. He begins to feel the ever increasing pressure of the provider. Tennis lessons for Mark, braces for Stephanie, tutoring for Marcy all add up to more budget worries for Daddy. The priority of what *he* wants and needs may slip into second or third or fourth place. And he will know it. Particularly if in the middle of an intimate time of snuggling you suddenly declare, "Marcy's math teacher is being such a pain. Do you want to go talk to her?" No, that is *not* what he wants at this immediate moment. Bad, bad timing. He can tell where your mind is–and it's obviously not in the loveboat with him!

The best thing you can do for your children is to love one another deeply, securely. In a world where they see their friends' families faltering and failing, your children can know the stability of loving continuity. Protect them from the fear of divorce by openly showing them how much you love each other. Give them that bedrock security.

ALONE AT LAST

There comes another changepoint in life where priorities tend to shift. When your last little fledgling has finally been launched from the nest, you will undoubtedly face a crucial time. Suddenly there are just the two of you. Alone at last.

This can be a wonderful time. Now you can do all those things together that you never had the hours or energy or funds for before. But a kind of chaos seems to overtake many women at this juncture of life. Rather than sitting back to enjoy the peace and quiet which they have earned, many rush into a frantic flurry of activity to fill the empty hours. One dear lady quickly brought another fledgling into her nest, a disturbed foster child who added nothing but grief. Another marched headlong into a full-time college career, taking seventeen hours her first semester. She was overwhelmed, having forgotten her study skills over the years. Another decided to go into real estate sales "to make all the money in the world I can make and finally do something on my own." Still another flies all over the country attending every seminar she can find because she feels God has a special ministry for her. Never mind that her husband is unhappy she is gone so much.

MAKE TIME FOR YOU

The common denominator here seems to be that when women reach this point in their lives they think, "There is finally time for *me!*"

What a sad way to live. All of us need "time for me" right now. Not at some future date out there we can point to and dream about. Right now.

"But right now I'm just a bride learning how to be a wife . . ."

"But right now I'm a tired mother with another new baby to care for . . ."

"But right now I'm driving carpool to three different schools, dance lessons, and soccer practice . . ."

Every bride, every new mother, every homemaker, every single one of us needs some inviolate time each week which is "just for me." God never asked you to become a living sacrifice to the demands of your family.

Make time in your life for *you*. Your desires. Your dreams. You do not have to put them on hold for twenty years until your nest is empty. Take that art class now. Learn to play the violin. Study French. What is it that you dream about for some future day? Begin now. Even if it is just a small beginning at least it is a start. Your family will benefit from your own feeling of satisfaction.

One of my friends used to leave her three small children in a Mother's Day Out program once a week. Guess how she used her time. She drove home, took the phone off the hook, got out a favorite book, and immersed herself up to the neck in a tubful of bubbles! That was what she needed to revitalize her emotions and refresh her soul.

Whatever it is you need to keep yourself vital and alive—do it now. Do not smother yourself so totally in the needs of your family that when you finally do have time for yourself you want to fly directly opposite of the way you have been living for years. Your husband will be alarmed by the sudden swerve in behavior. What is happening to his lover, his wife, his sweetheart? Why is she suddenly so "me-centered"? It can be a bewildering time for both of you if you hit it with years of pent-up frustration of waiting for "time for *me*."

"This above all, to thine own self be true," wrote William Shakespeare, "and it will follow, as the night the day, thou canst not then be false to any man." Especially your own special man. Keep your priorities straight.

NEVER SETTLE INTO FRUMPY

This point must be emphasized again and again: A wife must always continue to be her man's girlfriend too. Never be willing to drift along contentedly settling into the frumpy housewife mold. It is most important to retain all through life those special attributes which attracted your husband in the first place.

Were you the bright, perky cheerleader type? Try to keep your enthusiasm for life. He needs that from you. It is part of why he chose you. My friend Sharon who has been married over twenty years and has four children recently went to her husband's high school reunion costume party wearing her cheerleader uniform from her own high school days! Are you impressed? I certainly was.

Perhaps you were the glamour girl or the dramatic type when you met your husband. Take a good long look at yourself. That glamour, that drama is still in there, maybe buried a little under the load of the intervening years. But you can still bring it out and surprise him this evening in little ways like you used to do.

What drew him to you? Were you the All-American, fresh-faced girl next door that everybody loved? Do you still greet him in that joyous "what's next" way? Do you still sing that special song for him? Reach back across the years to refurbish your "girlfriend" image. Remind him in ways he cannot miss that you are still that girlfriend he chose over all the others.

You see, to a man there is a difference, and the sirens of this world have certainly played on this difference. The wife is the good woman who keeps a man's house, budgets his money, raises his children. Ah, but the *lover* is the glamorous one he takes to fancy places, brings frilly presents, and finds his pleasure with. Too often in our world these two people are two separate women. In the Kingdom of God, these two images must be contained in the same frame. You.

Quite a challenge, is it not? Part of loving your husband is to keep the excitement in your marriage. Keep him in love with you and loving you. Yes, be his faithful wife, while you also are his lover. Do not allow the cares of marriage, such as problems with children, in-laws, bills, to weigh you down. He needs to see in you the buoyancy of joy and excitement and romance that brought the two of you together. "Impossible!" you say? Not if you really desire this. We always make time for the things we really want to do. Perhaps it is simply a matter of moving your husband back to the top of your priority list. Has he slipped down a notch or two lately?

Become his girlfriend again. Tell him you want a date with him, just the two of you, at least once a week. He may be surprised, even astounded, but secretly he will be pleased, because down deep inside he still sees himself as that young, handsome guy who won you. Our husbands are told to "rejoice in the wife of your youth," and furthermore, "may you ever be captivated by her love." (Proverbs 5:18,19) We wives must give our husbands ample opportunity to fulfill these instructions from the world's best handbook on marriage.

We must be their love covering. Our husbands should be so fulfilled by our loving at home that they are never lured by a worldly siren. Succinct advice my mother offered me, "If you feed him steak at home, he won't go off for hamburger somewhere else." A harmonious sex life is of utmost importance.

Beyond the bedroom intimacy, take delight in daily affection: touching, hugging, encouraging, caring, stroking. Rub his back in private and stroke him with your words in public. Help others notice the good in him. "My husband did the sweetest thing today . . ." "Honey, tell that great story you know about . . ." Then please don't ruin it all by interrupting him or correcting him.

BUILDING, NOT DEMOLISHING

Does it nettle you to see couples sniping at one another? "Better to live on a corner of the roof than share a house with a quarrelsome wife." (Proverbs 21:9) Have you seen a wife who constantly puts her husband down, even under the guise of teasing? "The wise woman

67

builds her house, but with her own hands the foolish one tears hers down." (Proverbs 14:1) Let us be sure we are building, not demolishing.

KEEPING YOUR HOME A CASTLE

Speaking of building our houses, we must keep in mind the old adage "A man's home is his castle." Every man needs to be lord of his domain, even if that domain is but a tiny garage apartment. He needs to be made comfortable there, to be warmed and welcomed at the end of his long, tiring day. His home should be a place of peace which he looks forward to entering, not a battlefield he dreads. He ought to have a particular place that is his alone. Depending on the amount of space available, it could be an entire room filled with all his favorite things (including those tacky deer horns) or simply a comfortable old chair in a quiet place with his newspaper on the table nearby. Remember that it is his place, his space. You do not need to straighten it, move it, or improve it. Just leave it alone. When he wants it changed, he will change it. He needs a place that is his alone, to do with as he chooses.

Too many times we busy little nestbuilders think we have to have the entire house just to suit us. If that means tossing out his worn old armchair, then out it goes! No, no. Bad choice. If that chair really is an eyesore, you can gently discuss replacing it or at least restoring it with some new fabric. Keep in mind who is out there slaving away everyday to bring home the paycheck so that we can afford to feather our nests. He is. So by all rights he should have the most comfortable spot he can find in which to unwind at the end of his long day.

That was something my uncle never had, and I often wondered why. If anybody deserved it, he did.

I was most blessed to grow up within a big family of aunts, uncles, and cousins. We were a closeknit family, often in and out of one another's homes. So I saw quite a variety of family life up close. Some of my uncles married "up" and some of my aunts married "down," providing quite a spectrum of life to my observant eyes.

This particular uncle was a great favorite of mine. He was a strong, gentle, handsome man who loved kids and dogs. I suppose he must have loved his wife too, although I never saw my aunt give him any affection. Theirs was a strange, fascinating household. My uncle brought home a substantial paycheck which he turned over totally to my aunt. She kept him on an "allowance" of $20.00 a week. With the rest of the money, she bought fine furniture, sterling silver, Irish linens, beautiful china, the first piano I ever remember seeing in someone's home, an intricate gold and crystal anniversary clock. Lovely things.

But this was the strange part: All those beautiful brocade chairs were covered with tattered quilts "to protect them." Even the lampshades kept their plastic covers on. Nobody knew how to play the piano or even took lessons to learn. The silver was hidden away somewhere. The fancy linens and china never graced the table. In fact, I cannot remember sitting down to a meal in the dining room. We always ate at the kitchen table. And my uncle never seemed at ease in his own home. Immediately after supper he would take the table scraps out to feed his hunting dogs. He'd stay out there all evening, petting them, talking to them until bedtime.

I used to think my uncle loved those dogs of his more than he loved his wife and kids. Maybe he did. Come to think of it, the demanding way his wife and kids treated him, perhaps he spent his evenings in the most pleasant company available. This kind man deserved better than he got, yet I never once heard him complain. And I loved him for it.

FROM HIS POINT OF VIEW

Try to see things from your husband's point of view once in a while. Suppose he works in loud surroundings all day, such as an airport or factory. How do you think he would like to be greeted when he comes home? With a warm hug, some soft music, his children

69

playing quietly, and dinner fragrantly waiting in the oven? Or with the TV blaring out the "Evening News" catastrophes, his children shrieking about whose turn it is, and you tied up on the telephone?

Suppose he works very closely with people all day long, in a sales force or schoolroom or supervisor's station. Perhaps he is under great stress at work with a critical boss always demanding more and still more from him. Maybe the field he is in has taken a real downturn in the economy lately. When he comes home, he may need some space for a while. He is not shutting you out. He just needs a little alone time to untangle the knots of the day.

If you can see things from his point of view, you will think twice before greeting him with, "Why are you late? We have to be at the Allen's in ten minutes flat–so hurry up!" or "Jimmy has been a brat all day and I told him you were gonna spank him the minute you walked in the door."

When you know he has been handling pressure all day long, please do not dump another load on him. If he has had to make ten thousand decisions in his job today, don't ask him what you should fix for dinner. If he has been working with intricate machines for hours, he does not want to figure out what's wrong with the microwave. Wait a while.

HELP FROM A GRACIOUS WIFE

A loving wife is a helper to her husband, not a hindrance. That is God's stated purpose for our creation. (See Genesis 2:18) He saw that man needed love, comfort, help. Man was given tremendous responsibility delegated by God Himself, and he needed help to fulfill his charge successfully. Things have not changed for man in all the thousands of intervening years. He still needs love, comfort, and help from a gracious wife. Take a good look at any successful man today. In almost every case you will find a wife who has stood right beside that man during his long climb to the top, encouraging, sacrificing when necessary, never competing, always completing.

GOD BRINGS A BALANCE

It is fascinating to see how God puts two people together. Have you ever wondered about a certain couple? "What on earth did she see in him?" Or, "He could have had anybody, so why did he choose her?" Quite often opposites do attract, because God is bringing a balance into two lives when He links them as one. Vivacious, charming Trisha is married to shy, steady Bruce. She opens up his narrow world to new people, new experiences while he provides the stability and security she never had as a child. Spendthrift, happy-go-lucky Spencer needs the practicality and patience of pennywise Patti. But he brings surprises and delights into her life which she had never dreamed of.

As for me, I wanted a tall, handsome, blue-eyed blond husband. That was my pattern. My daddy, a tall, handsome, blue-eyed blond, was a wonderful husband to my mother. I also specifically told the Lord that I wanted my man to be a strong spiritual leader. God graciously gave me the desires of my heart.

BLENDING STRENGTHS AND WEAKNESSES

However, we often find that those very strengths in our mate which attract us are potential sources of conflict as we blend our two lives together. Her vivacious chatter which was so cute when they were dating can drive him crazy on a continual basis. His lovely surprise gifts which swept her off her feet when they were courting now take her breath away when she tries to balance the checkbook. As for me, I soon found that a strong spiritual leader heard directions from the Lord which often challenged my strong "But I know best!" mentality.

Hold on tightly. Just remember through all those initial ups and downs that you are weak where he is strong, so let him be strong. Also know there are places where he is weak and you can be the helper he has needed all his life. Your strengths and weaknesses blended perfectly with your husband's will create a bond to last a lifetime.

71

FOUR BASIC AREAS OF BALANCE

Check these four basic areas of balance in your marriage. They are all necessary to maintain a lifetime of togetherness.

Your spiritual life:

Do you pray together every day?
Do you encourage one another with promises from the Word of God?
Are you committed to a local church?
Do you share good books and inspiring testimonies with each other?
Do you seek God's guidance together for all your major decisions?

Your emotional life:

Do you recognize the areas of emotional need in one another?
Are you sensitive and gentle in these areas?
Do you realize that God put you together to balance one another?
Are you careful with your words in private as well as in public?
Are you free to show emotion in front of each other?

Your physical life:

Do you have a harmonious sex life?
If not, are you seeking help and counsel?
Do you keep yourself physically attractive for one another?
Do you fill your days with little caresses, lovepats, rubbing tired shoulders, lots of hugs?
Do you keep your home as pleasant as possible in all ways?

Your social life:

Do you still date one another?
Do you make sure there are weekly family fun times?

Do you make every effort to live at peace with your family-in-law?
Do you have friendships with couples which have lasted several years?
Are you aware of making lovely memories for one another?

THROUGH ALL THE TESTS OF TIME

The answer to each of these questions should be *yes*. If you
cannot answer them all affirmatively, seek the Lord's help in the particular area where you fall short. There may not be a real problem, just
a lack of diligence. Marriage must be nurtured like any other living
thing. Love. Time. Care. Understanding. Hope. Lavish these positive qualities on one another and your marriage will stand strong through
all the tests of time. You two *can* make it together.

On our twentieth anniversary, Robert took me out for a lovely
evening. Over candlelight and seafood, we remembered and laughed.
Our curious waiter finally commented on how happy we looked. He
asked if this were a special occasion. "Twenty years tonight," we told
him. The man shook his head in disbelief. "Twenty years! Wow, that
is something to celebrate. Not many marriages make it that far nowadays."

THE GOAL OF EVERY BRIDE AND GROOM

No, not in the world's way of marriage. But in the Kingdom
of God, marriages are holding strong. Robert and I have now celebrated over thirty years. One day we counted the years of lasting
bonds in our family. Just with his parents and mine and us, there are
over 130 years of love and fidelity. Beyond that we have a heritage of
faithfulness. Both sets of grandparents on both sides of our families
remained faithfully committed to each other all their lives. Robert has
two brothers and a sister, all of whom have continued in committed
marriages for 40 years. You can see in our family alone that marriages
can indeed last.

73

In fact, caring couples everywhere are holding on tightly to one another, honoring their covenant "until death do us part." Lifetime commitment must be the goal of every bride and groom who stand before the altar of God. In the eternal words of our Savior, "What therefore God hath joined together, let not man put asunder."

CHAPTER 4

TRAINING THEM UP

"to love their children"
Titus 2:4

When the distinguished actress Mercedes McCambridge came to Dallas for the play "J.B." (in which she played the part of the devil) she made the most astounding remark: "I scorn prayer. I scorn the Church's teachings. And I scorn a whole bunch of stuff. But let me have a toothache, or let me worry about a sound outside the door at night, and I go right back to *Our Father, who art in heaven . . .* Right back to it."

Is that amazing or what?

It points up the fact that all our years of worldly sophistication, education, and philosophy are simply a veneer covering the little child within us. No wonder the Word commands, "Train up a child in the way he should go: and when he is old, he will not depart from it." (Proverbs 22:6 KJV) The Lord knows that when we lay the foundation of righteousness in our young child's soul he will have the bedrock of faith to support him when all else fails.

This is a prime reason why mothers need to stay at home with their young children. No one else will love that child the way you do. No one else will train him in righteousness like you can. No other person can instill in him your own priceless set of values. Nobody else is Mother.

A CHILD LEFT TO HIMSELF

Yet in our world today, a great many mothers leave the training of their children to daycare centers or schools or churches. Countless numbers of parents have walked away from their responsibility to "train up" their own child. Eighteen years later these parents cannot fathom why this same child rejects their entire set of values, "When we've worked so hard to give him every advantage!"

They could find the reason for such rejection in Proverbs 29:15, "A child left to himself bringeth his mother to shame." (KJV) How accurate is the picture drawn here. A child left to himself. Without guidance, without nurturing, without discipline. This child is headed for disgrace.

Fervently I urged an acquaintance not to leave her daughters at home while she traveled abroad for extended ministry meetings. "But my girls are old enough to care for themselves. One is fifteen, the other twelve," she countered. "Besides, God has charged me with bringing this message of repentance to the Church. I must go where the door opens and trust Him to care for my family."

Although she was sincere and sounded very pious, this mother was moving totally outside of God's divine order for her family. Imagine her trauma when she returned from ministry abroad to find her own daughter facing sexual molestation charges. This girl had taken out her resentment on the children she babysat. How tragic. A child left to herself brings her mother to shame. A child left to herself strikes out against the absent parent in ways one never dreamed.

The arguments ring out from bewildered parents: "But we gave them the best of everything! Designer clothes. Straight teeth. Private school."

"We sheltered them in a lovely home. Each child had his own room, a special place to entertain his friends. Color-coordinated, with all the latest video/Nintendo/whatever-o."

"We sacrificed to give her every advantage—tennis lessons, dance classes, summer camps. We pushed her toward success . . ." On and on and on.

But, "a child left to himself bringeth his mother to shame."

QUANTITY OF THINGS OR QUALITY OF TIME?

How did we ever come to gauge our parenting by the quantity of *things* we give rather than the quality of *time* we give? Our time is our most precious asset, for time can never be replaced. Once spent, it is eternally gone. Those hours you spend with your child are an investment in the security of his personhood. He knows he is valuable because you choose to be with him. He is secure in your love for him quite simply because of all those hours you spend playing silly games, munching crisp apples, reading "The Little Engine That Could" (again!), swinging him at the park, explaining why cats have long tails and dogs have long ears.

These seemingly trivial strands of togetherness stretch across the days and years to weave a security blanket of love which will comfort your child when the cold winds blow. Today, however, this quality of mothering is in short supply. Single parent households are a stark fact of life. Mother must work to put bread on the table. Each month she hopes against hope that the child support check will come.

In those homes where both parents work, Mother is able to provide some extra "advantages" but very little caregiving. Yet the bottom line of life for children is that they need care. Consistent, nurturing care.

Child development specialists look to the future of today's children with real concern. They know that children must have a primary constant caregiver in the first years of life, particularly in infancy, to create the bonding mechanism of their emotions. Bonding is what holds together all relationships, that intangible attachment deep within the soul.

Yet thousands of infants are left daily in care centers which are little more than warehouses for children. Currently over 50% of children less than one year old are left in daycare. And this number continues to climb. These babies' waking, learning, growing hours are presided over by hired caregivers who come and go, here today and gone tomorrow to better paying jobs. How dreadful it is that our most valuable national resource, our children, are being cared for by our lowest paid workers. Even the most dedicated childcare worker must face economic reality. She cannot remain forever in such a low paying job.

So Baby Jeffry, who has come to love Miss Nancy because she cuddles him every day, arrives at Tiny Tot Warehouse #47 on Tuesday morning to discover that his beloved Miss Nancy has disappeared. In her place a Miss Sally is now feeding and changing him, but she doesn't cuddle him like Miss Nancy did. He soon finds that Miss Sally is kind in her own way, and so he comes to love her too, for a while. Then one Friday morning when Mom drops him off, Baby Jeffry looks up to find Miss Sally gone. Who is this Miss Linda? Where did she come from? How long will she be here?

In most daycare settings, there is not one constant primary caregiver for a child to bond with. So the child's tender little emotions learn early on that he cannot trust the one who cares for him simply *to be there*. He decides not to get too attached to any one caregiver lest he suffer continuous loss.

THE DAYCARE GENERATION

What effect will such bonding impairment leave on this generation?

Will children be able to form lasting marriage commitments?

Will they even want to?

No one knows. We can only take a "wait and see" stance to watch the outcome of modern history's first daycare generation. A great many of these young people will probably choose to remain single. Those who do marry may have a high divorce rate because they never learned to bond to one person. A bleak prospect at best.

The ideal situation, of course, is for Mother to stay at home and create the bonding relationship her children need. If that is not possible because you are the only breadwinner, then pray for God to help you find a constant caregiver who will really love your child. It must be someone with your own values, someone with whom you can share the mothering bond. That main bond will form with the person who cares for your child on a daily basis. The one who teaches pattycakes, makes the peanut butter sandwiches, kisses the scraped knees, shows how to color inside the lines, spends time laughing over the puppy's antics, crying over the hurt feelings, living and learning and growing.

Perhaps you are the one who will offer nurturing to a child who would otherwise be warehoused. So many children today face this warehouse situation because there is no other alternative when their parents divorce. Mother is thrust into the marketplace, trying to deal with her own rejection by a husband she once loved. If you see this situation, and God leads you to be part of the solution, you will have a major impartation into the life of a child who needs day to day nurturing.

THE PRIORITY OF QUALITY CAREGIVING

I salute all of you women who are providing homecare for those children whose mothers must work or choose to work outside their home. The money you receive in exchange for the nurturing you give can in no way measure the value of what you are doing.

I salute you for opening your home and heart, for being a daily living example of love.

All of you thousands of young mothers who have stepped out of careers into the priority of quality caregiving, I salute you. As Abraham Lincoln said, "The hand that rocks the cradle rules the world." Time alone will show you how all-important is your decision to sacrifice. To cook hamburger 101 ways. To make do with the old carpet. To stay at home and give time, attention, and affection to your little ones. They will not remember that the dining room chairs were mismatched. But they will fondly recall the birthday party where you covered the table with red and white balloons and brought the puppy in to help blow out the candles.

A FOUR-PART STRATEGY

Training children to become whole, well-adjusted adults is a full-time occupation in itself. There are many wonderful books devoted entirely to this subject. Therefore, I will only discuss what I consider the four basic areas of good training. Your tactics may vary but your strategy must include:

love,
guidance,
discipline,
instruction in righteousness.

PART ONE: LOVING OUR CHILDREN

First and foremost, let's talk about loving our children. After all, love and Jesus are the most important elements of life that we can give them. Love never fails. Nor does Jesus.

When my son Kipling was growing up, his Grandmother Holder would say of this, her only grandchild, "If love will keep that precious one on the right track, we never have to worry about his future. He is one loved little boy." Indeed, Kip has matured into a godly, secure young man because of all that love and Jesus.

One day when he was about seven years old, he was playing with a neighborhood buddy in his room. Passing by the door, I caught the friend's remark. "Jesus, Jesus, Jesus. That's all I ever hear in this house. Is that *all* your folks ever talk about?" I froze in midstride to catch Kip's response. Would he be defensive? Embarrassed? Try to explain? Not at all. Very matter-of-factly he replied, "Jesus, Jesus, Jesus. Yep, that's about it." And that was that.

Other young people I have known across the years have confessed, "It was my mother's love that kept me on the right track. She loved me so much I would never do anything to bring shame to her." What a testimony to the keeping power of a mother's love.

Danny was going through some teenage rebellion when he told me, "I wish I could ditch it all—school, church, everything—and just head out on the open road with my thumb and my backpack."

"So, what's keeping you here?" I asked.

A resigned sigh, then "My mom. She loves me so much I can't just blow it all off. If I started wandering around God-knows-where, I'd worry Mom to death. I can't do that to her."

I smiled inwardly. Mother's love triumphs again.

LEARNING TO LOVE

However, some mothers have never learned how to love their children. Learned how? You would think that loving your child would come as naturally as breathing. After all, you have been expectantly waiting nine long months for this little pink bundle to arrive. You spent hours and hours, not to mention every extra dime to transform the spare room into a beautiful Babyland. You agonized over pastels or bright colors. You pored over the book "1001 Names and What They Mean" to choose the perfect name for what will surely be the perfect child. You have consoled yourself that swollen ankles, swollen fingers, indeed swollen everythings will be worth it all when that precious little angel arrives.

As indeed it is.

Then reality kicks in. The little angel wants to eat every two hours of every day and every *night*. When the meal is slow in coming, her tiny face screws up, turns beet red, and she caterwauls a most unangelic howl. You now think of Heaven as a place where you could have ten uninterrupted hours of sound sleep. You cannot believe any baby could go through so many diapers in a single day. You wish you had bought stock in the Pampers company.

Then one night she sleeps the whole night through. You wake with a start, jump up and run to see if she's still breathing! There she is in her crib, cooing and burbling, enjoying the dawn, letting Mommy sleep awhile longer. What a little darling! What an angel! Motherhood is marvelous.

Yes, it is. It really is. In fact, children are a reward from the Lord. (Psalm 127:3) And He knows just the type of child to send you. Take comfort from that, Mom, when your strong-willed child is driving you up the wall. God gave him to you. God will also give you the wisdom and grace to handle him with love.

A NEW FAMILY PATTERN

We need God's love poured through us to our children, for human love is not enough to sustain us in the difficult times. If love from our own parents was meager or even withheld, we must depend totally on God's grace to establish a new family order through us for the lives we have brought into this world.

It *can* be done. People can break the chains of despair and misery and rejection that they suffered as children. They can grow up to be loving, nurturing parents who transform their bleak past into bright hope for their own children. It simply takes God's supernatural power to break that generational curse, to begin a new, loving family pattern.

Parents, the greatest gift you can give to your children is to love one another. Really love each other deeply and let your children know it. That will build stability into them more than anything else you can ever do for them.

I am reminded of hearing Kip once declare to someone on the phone, "No, that will never happen to my folks. They really love each other. I never wake up in the night to hear them yelling or fighting. They will always stay together because they love each other, and they love me." Simple and settled.

A HUG, A SQUEEZE, A SMILE

Let there be an open display of affection in your home. Lots of hugs for everyone. Kiss your family when they come in and pet them before they go out. Cuddle the kids every day—little kids, big kids, grown kids. No touch is like Mom's touch. Stroke your daughter's hair. Rub your son's back. Pat her cheek. Smile and wink at him. Pull her onto your lap. Squeeze his muscles and admire. Give them your time, attention, and affection.

It is important for each child in the family to have some time with you that is especially his own. This may be harder to achieve in large families, but it is worth the extra effort. When children know they will have their own special time with Mama, they will feel less need to vie for her attention. Also, this will assure that the rambunctious child does not get the lion's share of your time while the quiet one is deprived.

TUCK IN TIME

We found "tuck in time" to be the perfect quiet time together. At evening's end we would look back over the day's events and count our blessings or make amends, as need be. Sometimes we read a favorite story. Always we asked the Lord to help our son as he struggled with his childhood problems, like the bully down the street, or the stray kitten he saw, or the geography assignment he forgot. Then we would kiss him, tell him what a fine fellow he was and how proud of him we were, and leave him to fall asleep with our blessing lingering over his bed.

One summer night Kip wanted to sleep in the men's cabin at Wildwood School. This was a Christian vocational school for young adults Robert had founded. So I brought some sheets, made up one of the extra bunks, and sat down to tuck him in.

A couple of the students came drifting in just as we finished our sweet time together. "Aw, look at that," Steve pointed, grinning broadly.

"Now don't make fun," I replied. "After all, he's only eight years old."

To my surprise this burly young man quietly declared, "Me, make fun of being tucked in? Nope, not me. That's the best part of childhood."

Yes, that little bedtime routine was very special to us. Even as Kip grew into his teenage years and began to set his own bedtime schedule, he would still come poke his head around the door to say, "Ready, Mom." Though much too grown up to admit it, he was really saying, "It's tuck-in time."

THE BEDTIME BATTLE

This way of ending your child's day is imminently more satisfying than the battle royal which many parents endure.

"Mommy, I need a drink of water."

"You have already had two drinks. No more."

"Then I need to go potty."

"No, you don't. You just want to get up again. Go to sleep."

"Mommy, I'm hungry. Can I have a cookie?"

"Elizabeth Ann, go–to–sleep!"

"I'm scared, Mommy. Come here, please, please, p-l-e-a-s-e . . ."

The light snaps on to display a frustrated Mommy whose patience is wearing thin.

"Read me another story?" wheedles the child.

"Listen, little girl, you have had a bedtime drink. You have had a bedtime story and a bedtime kiss. You have had a bedtime snack. Now if I hear one more word out of you, you're gonna get a bedtime smack!" The light shuts off, the door slams, closing darkness down over a whining child and an exasperated mom.

SET THE BEDTIME BOUNDARIES

As the parent, it is up to you to set the bedtime boundaries. If it has become a constant struggle with your child, now is the time for you to take charge, to change the situation. Tell your child, with conviction ringing in your voice, "Tonight we are starting something special at bedtime, just you and me and Jesus. We'll read your favorite book. We'll say your prayers. And then we'll tuck you into your soft, warm bed. After our special time, I want you to go right to sleep. No more talking. No more getting out of bed. Just a nice, sleepytime trip to Dreamland."

Then carry out your plan. She may call you fifteen times, just to see if you will give in. Do not, repeat *not* throw up your hands in defeat and lose the battle. You might look in on her one time to make sure everything is alright and firmly declare, "I meant what I said. I love you, little precious girl. And it is time for you to sleep." Calmly, lovingly smile and walk away.

Sooner or later your child will come to treasure her tuck-in time. She will realize that it is her own very special time with Mommy or Daddy. She won't know why, but that few minutes will help her face the darkness of night. She will feel the lingering radiance of love protecting her.

87

GIVE THE SPECIAL TIME NOW

Whether you choose tuck in time or some other space of time for your child, it is important to begin now. So many people ignore the present while planning for the future. We plan to take our child on that special fishing trip. We plan for the vacation at the beach. We plan and plan for the future, never noticing day after day slipping by when we have given them no special time at all. Days melt into weeks, then into months. The fishing trip gets postponed. The vacation is put on hold for lack of funds. One day we realize they are suddenly grown up and we have almost lost touch with them. In a panic we clutch for them, only to find they have learned to live without us.

"How was your day, Kevin?"

"Same as always."

"Anything happen at school?"

"Not really. Why?"

"Oh, I just wondered. How about a game of chess after supper? Or let's go over your homework."

"Not tonight, Mom. I'm gonna hang out with Chad. Some other time, maybe."

Maybe. Maybe not.

A TEST OF COMMITMENT

I remember the specific moment when the Lord pulled Robert up short concerning his lack of quality time with our son. My husband has always been a very loving, giving pastor to all the people God sends us. He gives generously of himself and his time. One desperate family had just come into our church. They were in the throes of turmoil. The man and wife were on their second and third marriage respectively, and the children of this "blended" family were blending about like oil and water.

Came the day of the great father/son campout Robert and Kip

had been planning for weeks. As they were packing their gear, Robert was interrupted by the phone's shrill summons. It was Mr. Chalk. "Pastor, you've got to come help me find Mike. He's run away again. He's been hangin' out with the wrong kind of guys, and I'm afraid he'll do somethin' stupid if we don't find him."

Robert had twice before gone searching for this wayward teen-ager and convinced him to give the family situation a little more time to heal. Now Mike was gone again and here was the stepfather insisting it was the pastor's job to go find him. Robert explained that he already had plans for the evening. But the upset man demanded that the pastor's first duty was to his lost sheep. Finally Robert gave in.

As he replaced the receiver, Robert slowly turned to his waiting son. "Kip, I'm so sorry. We'll have to postpone our camping trip. There's a big problem. You see, Mike has run off again, and I've got to go help find him."

Kip hung his little head. "Daddy," he said sadly, "would you pray that I'll get a problem?"

"What do you mean, Son?"

"Well, you only spend time with people who have problems. So I need a problem so you'll spend time with me."

That simple plea pierced Robert's heart. He dropped to his knees, enfolded his son in his arms, and asked for forgiveness. Then he picked up the phone, called Mr. Chalk back, and said he must honor his prior commitment to his own son. He offered to send one of our young deacons who had found Mike before. Robert stiffened as the string of profanity which hurtled back across the line almost turned our phone blue. It audibly pointed up the fact that runaway Mike was not that family's main problem. Robert held firm and hung up. Then he turned to our son, secure in his decision. "Come on, Hoss, let's go camping."

Time. How important it is in the relationship with our children. The "law of the harvest" principle works in relationships too. If we allow everything to push in ahead of time with our children, we cannot expect a harvest of filial affection in our older years after they are grown. Plant the seeds of time and love in their little lives now to reap a harvest of continuous honor and caring throughout their adult years.

PRAYER, AS NATURAL AS BREATHING

Another area of vital importance in the realm of loving your children is the amount of prayer you lift to the Lord on their behalf. Pray for them every day, perhaps several times a day. "Pray without ceasing." (I Thessalonians 5:17 KJV) The battle for a quality life is won in prayer. Never let prayer be a stranger in your home. Keep it as natural, as regular as breathing.

Pray before meals.

Pray before bedtime.

Pray before they leave for school.

Pray before they hit the football field.

Pray for them in any defeat.

Cover your children with prayer. When you see temptation wooing them, pray a "hedge of thorns" about them to keep them from stumbling into harm's way. (See Hosea 2:6 KJV.) Let them know you are praying this way. It works. God seems to hold a special place in His heart for a mother's prayer.

Every child needs a wholesome fear of God. "The fear of the Lord is the beginning of wisdom; all who follow his precepts have good understanding . . ." (Psalm 111:10)

I tried to instill a holy fear of the Lord into Kip by letting him know I had prayed that he would get caught if he ever tried to do wrong. He believed me because he put it to the test a couple of times, only to discover that God indeed was listening to his mother's prayers.

How did I know it would work? My own mother did the very same thing for me. Yes, *for* me—not *to* me. It was a tremendous blessing to finally realize that the Lord cared enough to rein me in before I plunged headlong into disaster. Could I cheat on a test because I didn't take time to study? Forget it. I would get caught, sure as the world. Kids on both sides of me could cheat right under the teacher's nose. But not JoAn. If my eyes so much as strayed over to my friend's paper, I would look up to find the teacher's gaze boring right into my guilty face. How wonderful! If you learn you cannot cheat in little ways, you grow up to ignore temptations in big ways.

Another way to pray for your children is to set a "wall of fire" around them as protection from the enemy. (See Zechariah 2:5.) The destroyer has no weapon powerful enough to penetrate God's wall of fire. It is mighty protection for your family.

Still another way to pray is to cover everyone you love with the blood of Jesus. Just as God's people were spared from the Death Angel when they covered their doorposts with the blood of the Passover lamb (see Exodus 12) so today we have protection through the blood of Jesus Christ, our Passover Lamb slain on Calvary. Sin cannot pass through the blood of Jesus. So cover your loved ones with a mighty spiritual covering.

COVERED AND READY TO GO

Kip's first long journey away from us was a trip to the World's Fair in Knoxville, Tennessee. His best friend Marc had invited him to go along on their family vacation. Kip really wanted to go with the Henleys. They were fine people and would certainly take good care of him. Besides, he was almost fourteen years old. But 1200 miles away?

His bags were packed. The Henleys were coming for him in ten minutes. So we sat him down in the living room and began to pray. We covered every potential hazard with the blood of Jesus. We prayed the wall of fire to protect him from all harm and danger. Accidents, food poisoning, arguing in the car, flat tires, hurt feelings, lost money, lack of sleep, any and all viruses, disappointments, forgetting things, obedience, you name it—we covered it in prayer. As the Henley car pulled up in our driveway, Kip looked at us and wryly commented, "I

guess I'm ready to go. I'm covered for everything but an IRS audit!"
Yes, he returned safely. Yes, he had a marvelous time. And I
was grateful for this practice run of "letting go" when five short years
later he was called to travel into Russia with a missionary. My
heartstrings then had to stretch all the way to the Kremlin. But the
same faithful God who watched over Kipling at a World's Fair, USA,
was there to guide and protect him through the darkness of then Com-
munist USSR.

These are spiritual principles which have very practical
outworkings in our natural world. Try them. You will be delighted to
find how these prayers work. The hedge of thorns. The wall of fire.
The blood of Jesus.

A mother's prayer
Is ever there
Before God's throne
To call her own
Into His care.
Her mercy prayer
Surrounds that one,
Her precious son:
"Lord, keep him true
And close to You.
And for his life
A faithful wife
With joyful days
And godly ways."

PRAYING FOR LIFETIME CHOICES

While you are praying for your child, remember to include
that one who will become part of your family by marriage. Begin now
to bless him/her with the loving grace of the Lord as he/she grows up.

The song Wayne Watson sings, "Somewhere in the World," says it all:

And I don't even know her name,
But I'm praying for her just the same,
That the Lord will write His Name on her heart.
For somewhere in the course of his life
My little boy will need a godly wife,
So hold onto Jesus, Baby, wherever you are.

There are two vital, lifetime decisions your child will make. First, will he accept Jesus Christ as his Lord and Savior? And second, whom will he choose to marry? Your prayers can directly affect both choices.

A STRANGE SENSE OF PROTECTION

The late Don Basham wrote this poignant story in one of his newsletters: My wife Alice prayed for each unknown spouse our children would marry. Through the years, one by one, each child chose a fine, godly partner. Our youngest son-in-law, David, who grew up in a fatherless home in Brooklyn, New York, became involved with drugs as a teenager. While a number of his friends ended up in jail or dead from a drug overdose, somehow David escaped serious trouble. After finding the Lord and marrying our Laura, David shared how even during the bad years he always had a strange sense of God's protection. Alice told him why he may have felt that way. "David," she said, "we have prayed regularly for you since you were a small child." We didn't know how deeply David was moved until a few days later. The florist arrived at our door with a dozen lovely yellow roses for Alice. With them was a card from David which read simply, *I never knew before who to thank.*

You may be the only one praying for that child who will eventually become part of your family. God knows who that special one is, and He will honor your prayers of protection and mercy. As a very real part of loving your children, begin now to pray for the one with whom he/she will fall in love.

A beautiful pattern of prayer for our children was lifted to God by King David on behalf of his son as the kingdom he had built was about to pass into Solomon's keeping: "And give unto Solomon my son a perfect heart, to keep thy commandments, thy testimonies, and thy statutes, and to do all these things, and to build the palace for the which I have made provision." (I Chronicles 29:19 KJV) I have often prayed this very prayer for my own son, "Lord, please give Kipling a perfect heart. Help him keep Your commandments, Your requirements. Let him accomplish all the good things You have set before him to do for Your kingdom."

DOZENS OF DAILY WAYS

If we truly love our children, we will consistently pray for them. Do we love them? Of course we do. Let us remember to show them in daily dozens of ways how much we love them:

Showing patience when his little story winds on and on and on with the most trivial details.

Showing tenderness when her feelings have been crushed by her playmates.

Showing kindness when he wags home a pitiful stray.

Showing no frustration when she tries so hard, but cannot quite grasp how to tie those shoestrings.

Showing goodness even in stressful times of discipline.

Love your child for who he is, not for what he has done. He may never make starting lineup on the football team, especially if he is in a big city school competing against hundreds of boys. She may not be able to understand trigonometry, even though it was a breeze for you. He may resolutely refuse to join the youth choir even though he has a marvelous voice. She will likely contest your choice of clothes for her even though you know that peach is her very best color. None of these little disappointments must be allowed to make you withdraw your love from that child. Remember, he is himself, a unique individual, not an extension of your own personality. He needs your love and approval because of his own innate worth, not because he has lived up to your measuring stick.

WARM FUZZYS OR COLD PRICKLYS?

Children whose parents withhold love grow up to be severely damaged in the realm of self-esteem. Children *crave* approval and attention. If they do not receive it in a positive way, they will learn negative ways to demand your notice. Do you give your children warm fuzzys or cold pricklys? That is, do you stroke them with loving words or crush them with criticism?

Children learn what they live. The way we behave in everyday life is the living pattern they will have set in their minds. Sobering, but true.

If a child lives with criticism
    he learns to condemn.
If a child lives with hostility
    he learns to fight.
If a child lives with ridicule
    he learns to be shy.
If a child lives with shame
    he learns to feel guilty.
If a child lives with tolerance
    he learns to be patient.
If a child lives with encouragement
    he learns confidence.
If a child lives with praise
    he learns to appreciate.
If a child lives with fairness

he learns justice.
If a child lives with security
    he learns to have faith.
If a child lives with approval
    he learns to be himself.
If a child lives with acceptance and friendship
    he learns to find LOVE in the world.
                    —Dorothy Law Nolte

FOUR-PART STRATEGY
PART TWO: GUIDANCE

This brings us to the second area of good training for our children: Guidance. How are we training our children through the everyday behavior in our homes? Not the big moments where we all try to shine, but the day to day crises and triumphs that fill every mother's waking hours. What our children see consistently in our own behavior speaks more clearly than all the platitudes we can preach.

Good manners and good morals are caught, more than taught. We must set the example if we want our children to be kind, courteous, compassionate. What happens to our determination to "speak the truth in love"? (Ephesians 4:15) Does it evaporate under the daily stress of dealing with our children? How do you respond when Suzy spills her milk? With a clipped, hard edge in your voice, "Can't you ever learn to hold onto that stupid glass?" But children are small and glasses sometimes slippery.

GRACE AND COMPASSION

Mothers need God's grace to extend to their children. That is part of "training them up."

Think of your conversation with Craig the last time he came in

96

covered with scratches and scrapes. "I *warned* you about going down that hill on your skateboard. Do I have to take the dumb thing away from you? Are you gonna break your neck?" Instant replay would show the frustration crowding out compassion, impatience overruling tenderness. Click. That pattern sets in his tender mind.

Mothers need God's compassion to flow through them to their children. That is also part of "training them up."

Sometimes I wish I could hide a tape recorder in every home to capture the parent/child exchanges. What if someone had done that yesterday at your house? What kind of conversation would have been recorded? Loving, kind, compassionate? Harsh, shrill, biting? Cynical, sarcastic? Indifferent? Like it or not, your daily exchanges with your children are training them to respond either positively and gladly or negatively and poutingly. "The wise in heart are called discerning, and pleasant words promote instruction." (Proverbs 16:21)

We want our children to behave in an acceptable manner, to become contributing members of society. Therefore, we must draw out the boundaries of behavior and the guidelines of good taste for them.

THE BUILDING BLOCKS OF CHARACTER

What is important to you? Those are the things you will emphasize in your training. Godly character, certainly. Consideration for others. Obedience to authority. Compassion for the unfortunate. Truthfulness, courage, honor, loyalty, virtue. All the important building blocks of righteous character must be imparted to our children. They do not just flow out naturally from the human heart.

Beyond molding their characters, we will also train them in the things which are important to our family. They should know in any given situation, "Our family does not behave that way" or "Our family members always encourage one another to excellence" or "This is our family heritage, so we do things this way."

For example, our family likes a quiet home. Kip learned early on that he was not allowed to romp and stomp through the house. So often we have people in our home trying to find their way back to the peace of the Lord. Fragile hearts need a quiet place to heal. Intense emotions take time to vent. And shrieking children do not enhance an atmosphere of introspection.

But Kipling was a normal little boy who loved to run and jump and yell. He did plenty of that—in the proper place: outside in the yard or on the playground. Children can be taught to respect and enjoy the peace of your home.

Draw practical guidelines for them to follow, such as:

My bed is to sleep on, not to jump on.

That goes for our sofa too.

I eat with my spoon. I don't wave it or throw it or bang it.

I put my clothes and toys away. I like a clean room.

Matches are only used by grownups—always!

These guidelines are obviously for very young children. A good balance to remember is that you must provide as many "yes-yes" items as you have "no-no's." Otherwise their interesting world turns into one big No-land.

Little ones can learn to enjoy beauty without destroying it. Children love beautiful things, and they can be taught to touch gently. Please do not hide your lovely things away "so they won't get broken." Such an attitude deprives your child of the joy of a music box, the rich gleam of your silver candy dish, the wonder of a rainbow glancing off your crystal pitcher. Surround your children with beauty. Let it saturate their daily lives, so they will not be drawn off track by base things later on in life.

STIMULATE CREATIVITY

Encourage creativity in your child by making things with him. Give him toys that draw out creativity, such as building blocks, modeling clay, fingerpaint sets, and so on. Many adults buy toys that appeal to themselves but leave the child bored in ten minutes. Creative play is imminently satisfying to a child, for the desire to create something beautiful is a God-given quality.

Instill a love of good literature in your children by reading the children's classics to them. If you were not read to as a child, then you will thrill along with your children to C. S. Lewis's "Chronicles of Narnia." Or the wonderful old stories of "Black Beauty", "Five Little Peppers", "Lassie, Come Home." I recommend a wonderful guidebook, "Honey for a Child's Heart" by Gladys Hunt (Zondervan Publishers) to introduce you to the world of children's literature. Also, beautifully illustrated Bible storybooks are a must. Turn off the television and read a good book.

DRAWING OUT YOUR CHILD'S INTERESTS

Nowadays we must carefully monitor the television programs our children watch. I testified before a Congressional Subcommittee on my concern that today's programming is little more than thirty-minute commercials for the toys children will see in the stores. Many of the cartoon programs grow more occult every year. Do not let television desensitize your child.

I remember fondly teasing my Grandmother Darst because she would not allow a television set to be turned on in her presence. She called it "that old devil box." This was back in the innocent TV days of the '50's. Surely my grandmother was a far-sighted lady. The major onslaught against family time, manners, and morals has indeed come right into our homes through "that old devil box." Turn it off.

Many children turn on the television simply because they are bored. Provide alternate sources of play. Keep games, puzzles, and good records readily available. Draw out your child's interests. With Kip it was trains, locomotives, choo-choos. In fact, his first sentence was an excited "Choo-choo go bye-bye" as a train passed before us.

So we provided him with albums of train noises, conductor calls, and railway songs. We still laugh over snatches of songs that filled many hours in our son's early days. "Casey Jones, goin' to the Frisco, Casey Jones, with a lantern in his hand . . ."

One of Kip's little friends was interested in dinosaurs. Another was the great American outdoorsman, always wanting to set up a tent and camp out. Still another wanted to play Army every single day. You will see the direction your child's interest is developing. Nurture, guide, channel it into all the positive aspects. If it is Army, make it "the Army of the Lord."

A bored child is an unhappy person, and boredom can grow into a habit. The best cure for budding boredom is work. Have you taught your child to work? You know what is said about "all work and no play"? Well, the reverse is also true. All play and no work makes Johnny a spoiled brat. Every child needs some responsible work to do, beginning with picking up his toys as soon as he can toddle. The results should be rewarded with praise and approval.

As he grows older, his responsibilities should increase. And the rewards should keep commensurate pace. Only then will a child realize that his nice clothes and good food and warm house did not simply fall out of the sky. Someone had to work for them.

The absence of gratitude is a major problem with young people today. They have been given so much and had to work for so little. Most have never had to do without. Yes, sometimes their parents sacrifice in order to provide that new prom dress or sport wheels, but that is what they have been trained to expect. Most young people highly esteem the value of entertainment today, yet they disdain as drudgery the value of work.

RICHES TO RAGS

One millionaire's distressed wife came to me in tears. She had given her daughter the very best of everything: posh private school, beautiful designer clothes, her own beautifully decorated suite of rooms in the family mansion, a flashy red sportscar—everything! Yet this child was about to drive her mother crazy. The girl's expression was a perpetual pout. She flouted authority. She lorded it over the servants. She constantly criticized her mother and played her parents against one another. This sixteen-year-old was a mess.

"I'm thinking of sending her away to boarding school next year," the unhappy mother confessed. "I simply cannot handle another year like this one." I shook my head, thinking how all the years of pampering had brought this daughter to the place where she was unwelcome in her own home. Then that mother asked me a loaded question. "If she were your daughter, what would you do with her? Would you send her away?"

"Do you really want the truth?" I gently asked.

"Yes. I'm serious. What would you do?"

"My friend," I responded, "your daughter has never been required to give anything of herself. You have done everything for her. She thinks it is her Godgiven right to be wealthy, to order people around. Indeed, I would send her away for a while—but not to some exclusive boarding school. I would find the poorest missions work in the world and send her there. Perhaps she would learn a little about suffering and deprivation and caring."

They did it! Wonder of wonders, her parents sent this petted, petulant girl to work with a missionary in Calcutta, India! Talk about culture shock. That summer of service profoundly affected her life. She learned to work. She learned to give. She found she could bless others and relieve their suffering. She came back a completely changed person, so grateful for cleanliness, for toothpaste, so appreciative of air-conditioning, indeed of everything. The change in her was nothing short of miraculous.

Part of our guidance for our children must be allowing some lack in their lives. We cannot, must not give them everything they ask for. What they need, yes. What they merely want, no. A wise man once said, "At some time in his life every child should learn what it is to be hungry and have no food, to be cold and have no warm coat, to be lonely and have no one care. Only then can he appreciate the blessings of life."

Guide your child into gratitude. Train him to say "Thank you" for the smallest of things, as soon as he can talk. Teach him to write thank you notes as soon as he can write. Have daily prayers of thanksgiving to the Lord "who daily loadeth us with benefits." (Psalm 68:19 KJV)

LEARNING TO LISTEN

In order to keep the guidance mechanism in place during your child's teen years, you must begin early on to develop an atmosphere of openness between the two of you. Some children are naturally more reticent about their feelings, while others tell everything in their hearts. Just let your child continually know that you care how he feels, and whenever he wants to talk you'll be there to listen. Then listen.

We all-wise parents tend to jump in with judgment calls even before the child unburdens. Guard your tongue. Keep quiet until he is finished. Above all, do not react with shock or anger. That is the surest way I know to kill all communication with teenagers. In dealing with my own child and those I have taught over the years, I have learned to keep perfectly composed while listening to their tales of woe. Then, no matter if I feel like calling fire down from heaven on whoever has hurt them, I calmly probe the reasons behind the situation. Generally a young person can come to the right decision on his own if he is given the opportunity to talk it out.

KEEPING THE DISCUSSION DOOR OPEN

Once in a while I slip. That tends to happen when the subject is one I feel strongly about, such as the time Kip was discussing his friend's choice to wear an earring. This friend was not a female. Furthermore, this friend desired to minister to young people. I calmly began to explain why I felt that an earring on a man was totally out of place, linked him to worldly values, was a sign of rebellion, gave a poor example for young people to follow. The more I talked, the more adamant I became. Finally Kip said, "Mom, it's no big deal to him. In fact, he quit wearing one last year when his ear got infected."

"A sure sign of God's judgment," I declared.

"Oh, Mom, I *knew* you'd say that. As soon as the words were out of my mouth, I knew you'd say that. You are so funny about some things!" End of discussion.

It was left to my spiritual son Rod a few weeks later to calmly comment on why he felt it did not serve as a godly example for a man to wear an earring. Kip thoughtfully listened. The next week his friend's earring was gone.

Keep the lines of discussion open. Here are a few parental responses that are guaranteed to sever the connection:

"Because I said so, that's why!"

"I don't care if everybody *is* doing it—you're not everybody!"

"I said *no*, and that's final."

Retorts such as these, as well as others colored with our personal prejudices, slam the door on meaningful discussions with our children. Though they are almost grown, they still need our prayerful guidance. We must remember that the world they face is far more complex than our young days, more wicked, more removed from absolute morality. Let's continue to guide them back to God's Word for their decisions, remembering that He "has given us everything we need for life and godliness." (II Peter 1:3)

GUIDING INTO THE FACTS OF LIFE

One of the touchiest areas of guidance has to do with our child's developing sexuality. Sex education should be taught in the home by loving, unembarrassed parents. Most often it is left to schools and/or older kids to draw a totally distorted picture of this vital area of our lives. Then we wonder why so many Christian kids "get in trouble." Our children must know that our morality is Bible-based.

When your son or daughter begins to evidence interest in the opposite sex, give him/her a good Christian book that explains the facts of life from God's perspective. Read it together, and answer matter-of-factly any questions that arise. Sex is not dirty nor shameful. It is a wonderful gift God has created for marriage. Firmly explain that no matter what anyone says, how anyone pushes, the only reply to having sex before marriage is "No." Stay out of trouble. Keep your knees together and your hands in your lap.

Be sure you understand the question before you start handing out the answers. Did you hear the story about the child who asked, "Mom, where did I come from?" She had been wondering how to approach the subject, and now here it was upon her. She took a deep breath and carefully explained as much as she thought he could understand about the birds and the bees. "Now do you understand where you came from?" she asked. The child wrinkled up his nose. "Well, I guess so. But Billy told me he came from California, so I just wanted to know where I came from."

Lovingly, gently guide your children into God's grace and godly ways.

FOUR-PART STRATEGY
PART THREE: DISCIPLINE

Now we come to the third aspect of good training: Discipline.

First let me say that discipline is not a dirty word. Its very root is in the word "disciple." Your child is your disciple. You teach him how to behave, how to function in his world, how to relate to those around him. If you are a modern mother who believes in reasoning with your very young child rather than correcting him, you have some rough sledding ahead. Right now, before you go one more day through life, head for your nearest bookstore and buy a copy of Dr. James Dobson's "Dare to Discipline." It will set you free.

THE FORMULA FOR PERFECT PEACE

God's Word says, "Folly is bound up in the heart of a child, but the rod of discipline will drive it far from him." (Proverbs 22:15) Many parents feel this is an admonition to use a literal small rod on their child's bottom. Others think that this scripture means any consistent form of discipline. However you interpret it in your home, remember that consistency is the key. As the authority in your child's life, you represent God's authority. Unless he learns early in life to obey your authority, there is little reason to hope that he will obey the Lord's commands later on.

Perfect peace in the home is created by this formula: the right amount of discipline + the right amount of joy. Good discipline builds self-esteem into your child. He will know that you love him because you set boundaries for his protection. Of course he will test those limits. "Does Mom really mean that the stove is hot? Does she know best? W-a-a-a-h! I'd better listen to her next time."

Hebrews 12 has a very pointed discussion of discipline. In fact, the writer likens an undisciplined child to an illegitimate son. In other words, if we do not care enough about our children to discipline them, we are in essence setting them on a course bound for destruction. "He who spares the rod hates his son, but he who loves him is careful to discipline him." (Proverbs 13:24)

Godless media always portray anyone who spanks a child as an abuser. What nonsense! Let me make this perfectly clear: we are discussing correction here, not child abuse. Any wicked person who would batter a child will have to answer for such evil to God Himself. Of utmost concern to Jesus was the care for little ones. He gave strong warning to anyone who would harm a child. (See Matthew 18.)

Good discipline builds strength and hope into a child's foundation. If your son is allowed to get by with lies or tantrums, his foundation will soon be cracked with roots of deception and rebellion. "Discipline your son, for in that there is hope; do not be a willing party to his death." (Proverbs 19:18)

CONSISTENTLY AND LOVINGLY APPLIED

We must use God's principles for discipline. Anyone knows you cannot reason with a willful two-year-old, although I have seen plenty of mothers try. Lovingly applied correction on his little bottom will show quite clearly that mother knows best and expects obedience.

Let your child know exactly what you expect from him. His greatest *out* is, "Mommy, I didn't know. You didn't tell me." So spell it out for him: A, B, C. Get eye contact by lifting him onto your lap or bending down to his level. Make sure he hears you clearly and knows what you mean. Then follow up on what you said. Consistency is the real key here. Your child must know that good behavior is expected at all times. The same rules that apply at home also cover his actions at church, at friends' homes, in restaurants, in public places. If he discovers you will not correct him when he misbehaves in public, you can be sure of mischief every time you take him out.

When our Kip was about two years old, he began to try our patience every time we went into a restaurant. In traveling ministry, we endured restaurants as a necessary part of our lives, although I packed picnics as often as possible. Somewhere along the way, Kip simply decided he would no longer sit quietly in his highchair and eat his food. Instead, he fussed and fidgeted. He played with his dinner. He spilled his milk. He made a general nuisance of himself until finally Robert would pick up our defiant son and carry him outside to administer the needed correction. About halfway to the door, Kip would begin to repent loudly and wailingly, "No, Daddy, no! I be good boy, Daddy! Don't spank, Daddy!" Every eye in the place would fasten upon this six-foot-four father hauling his tiny son out the door. Yes, it was embarrassing. Certainly Kip knew what he was doing, pleading for mercy. Children instinctively know how to get sympathy. But the discipline was necessary to teach a toddler he was not in charge of our family. Robert would spank him, then love him, then bring a chastened little boy back to the table to finish our meal in peace. I cannot count the number of times this scenario was repeated. Finally Robert began to say, even before we entered a restaurant, "Kip, do you want me to go ahead and spank you now and get it over with?" Kip's eyes would grow big and round as he contemplated the question. "No, Daddy," he would solemnly reply, "I be good." And he was, and still is today.

ADMINISTERING BLESSING AND CORRECTION

There is no need to berate your child for his misconduct. Simply discipline him. No need to nag or threaten. Have you ever heard a busy mother trying to hurry along her dawdling little daughter (who is probably tired) by declaring, "Deborah Ann, if you don't hurry up and come on I'm gonna leave you right here in this big old store. Bye-bye. I'll come get you tomorrow." Many children take everything literally. They cannot distinguish between truth and teasing. Such idle threats only create fear of rejection or abandonment. Correction is needed here, not threats uttered out of Mom's frustration.

Please remember this: The hand is for blessing, the rod is for correcting. There is no excuse whatsoever to slap a child's face. In fact, if you become so angry with your child that you lose control, you thereby lose the right to correct him. Do you swoop down on your misbehaver like an avenging angel of doom? Do you pounce like a cat on a helpless mouse? No, never! Take time to cool off, repent before God for your anger, and settle things in your own heart before you deal with your child's shortcomings. Correction must always be done in love, never in anger. Angry correction only breeds rebellion in a child.

107

ACTION, NOT ANGER

It is *action*, not anger, which motivates a child to obedience. Your child knows where you draw the line, when you will take action. If Mom says, "Shane, leave the kitten alone," you can bet Shane knows exactly how many times he can touch that cat before his mother goes into action. His game is to push her right to the line of action—but not over. Once in a while Shane miscalculates his mother's patience, but most of the time he has her pegged exactly right.

Has this scenario ever been played out in your home? Your guest instructs her child, "Ashley, leave this candy dish alone." The minute Mom's attention is focused on you, Ashley tiptoes to the candy. "Ashley! Put that back this instant. I said, No candy." Ashley reluctantly places the chocolate drop back into the bowl. "Good girl. Now you leave it alone or I'll have to spank." Then Mother exits the room to see your new bedspread. As she oohs and aahs over your good taste, Ashley remains behind in the living room stuffing good tastes into her mouth. Suddenly your guest realizes her child is not with her, so she goes back to check on the ominous silence. Sure enough, chocolate-smeared Ashley, guilty and gooey, is caught in the act. She makes a funny face as she tries to choke down the rest of her loot before Mom grabs it. "You little clown," Mother laughs, "what am I going to do with you?" She snatches the candy bowl and puts it up out of reach, apologizing for the mess. Ashley registers three important facts:

1. Mom does not really mean what she says.
2. There are no real consequences to my disobedience.
3. If I look cute enough to make her laugh, I can get away with anything.

Keep your word, Mother. Do not warn and warn in a meaningless way. Two warnings are enough. Then take action.

Keep your word, Mother. Do not warn and warn, getting more upset with each warning until you explode into anger or dissolve into tears. Do not let your emotions get in the way of loving discipline. Ask for God's help. Realizing that He gave you this child should make you confident He will also grace you to handle him. Yes, even the strong-willed child.

OPPOSITE TEMPERAMENTS

I know whereof I speak, for I was a strong-willed child. By the time I was six years old, I had my whole neighborhood organized, deciding whether today we played Church or Cinderella or Leapfrog. And when I didn't want to do something, such as take my vitamins, I really dug my heels into the ground. I cannot recall how many spankings I got because of those dreadful vitamins. Since I was a puny child, I had a mother who insisted I take vitamins every single day. Thank God we now have delicious chewable vitamins for children. Back then they were nasty little red pills I had to swallow. I fought against swallowing them. I cried. I screamed. I spat them out. I clenched my teeth. I pushed my mother's patience to the limit—every day! What stubbornness. Finally she would have to spank me for my little tantrum. Then she would lovingly explain to me, once again, why it was necessary that I take my vitamin. Docile now, I would open wide, receive the little red pill, and swallow. And that was that, until the next day.

My younger brother had just the opposite temperament. His was such a tender heart that a harsh word would wound him. Thankfully, for Mother's sake, his discipline did not require such exertion. The mere expression of her disappointment in his behavior could bring tears of remorse to his eyes. On the rare occasions when he deserved a spanking, he would beseech me, "Pray for me, Sissy," as Daddy led him away.

You see, each child is unique, exquisitely formed as an individual by the Lord God Himself. Therefore, each will respond differently to discipline. There is no set formula that will work the same way with each child. You must be led by the Holy Spirit to give correction the best way in every individual case. Quite a challenge, yes? But very well worth all the time and effort you invest.

UNDER OUR ROOF, UNDER OUR RULES

How do you deal with disruptive children who belong to other people—for example, the little firecracker from next door who is always underfoot? I have taken the position that when a child is under my roof, he must conform to our house rules. If he starts swearing or jumping on the sofa or punching someone else, I gently but quite firmly let him know that no one is allowed to act that way in our home. "If you want to stay here and play with Kip, you must do as I ask. We love you, and we want you to be able to come here and play, so you must not beat on the piano (or throw the football across the room or whatever) like you've been doing. Next time you cause a problem, I'm sending you home. Do you understand?"

Often that is all it takes. Unruly children actually are crying out for guidelines, and they will usually respect your authority once you have made it clear. If the child is so spoiled that he totally disregards your word, then you must follow up with action. Send him home. Both he and your own child will see that you mean what you say. And I daresay the next time he comes over you'll find his attitude greatly altered.

CREATIVE DISCIPLINE FOR TEENAGERS

As our children grow older, our discipline must become more creative. It is most unwise to take a belt to a rebellious teenager to beat him into submission. That will simply drive him to further rebellion. "Fathers, do not exasperate your children; instead, bring them up in the training and instruction of the Lord." (Ephesians 6:4) "Fathers, do not embitter your children, or they will become discouraged." (Colossians 3:21) If we do bring them up in the training of the Lord, by the time they are teenagers our children will expect correction for unruly conduct. They will know that we require acceptable behavior. When the lines of communication have been kept open, our teens will likely be able to suggest what punishment we should mete out, even to the severity of it.

Be reasonable. Grounding a teenager for six weeks is like sending him to Siberia for a whole year. Make his punishment fit the crime. For example, if he took the family car without permission, insist that he fill the gas tank using his own money, wash and wax the car, then thoroughly clean and vacuum it inside. That is much more to the point than cutting off his allowance for two weeks. In other words, try to make the correction count for something. If she has abused her telephone privileges, she must sit down and write three encouraging letters to missionaries before she can use the phone again. If theft is involved, restitution must be made immediately by the child himself. Make him face the person he has wronged. Don't do it for him. Get it over and done with so your child can ask forgiveness, dispel the cloud of guilt, and get on with his life.

IN A SPIRIT OF LOVE

Most importantly, whatever his age, give all correction in a spirit of love without belittling your child. *Never* humiliate him before other people. When you recall the painful experiences of your own past, most of them will have something to do with damage to your self-esteem. Perhaps a bully taunted you in front of other children. Did a teacher belittle you before your classmates? Did a relative ridicule you with stinging remarks?

Once an exasperated mother told me, "This child wets her pants every time I turn around. Come on, Amy, let's go get you cleaned up again." Amy hung her head in shame. I was sad to have been the one to hear that pitiful confession. It didn't change a thing for Amy or her mother, except to further tarnish a little girl's self-image.

Father God, please help us as parents to realize that our child is a special person in his own right, not merely an extension of ourselves. Give us wisdom in all our dealings with these precious lives you have entrusted to our care. Help us to love them and guide them and correct them in ways that bring glory to You and godliness to them. Amen.

FOUR-PART STRATEGY
PART FOUR: INSTRUCTION IN RIGHTEOUSNESS

Finally, of paramount importance in training up our children is their Instruction in Righteousness. A wall hanging handcrafted by a friend shows our heart: "As for me and my house, we will serve the Lord. Joshua 24:15"

Fundamentally, Instruction in Righteousness is imparting our vision of Jesus Christ to our household. From the cuddly musical lamb that plays "Jesus Loves Me" in the crib continuing throughout all their lives under our care, it is imperative that we keep our vision of Jesus ever before them. The instructions Moses gave God's children thousands of years ago still hold true for God's children today, "Hear, O Israel: The Lord our God, the Lord is one Lord. Love the Lord your God with all your heart and with all your soul and with all your strength. These commandments that I give you today are to be upon your hearts. Impress them on your children. Talk about them when you sit at home and when you walk along the road, when you lie down and when you get up. Tie them as symbols on your hands and bind them on your foreheads. Write them on the doorframes of your houses and on your gates." (Deuteronomy 6:4-9)

In modern terms, completely saturate your daily life with the principles and Presence of the Lord Jesus Christ. Remind one another of how good the Lord has been to your family. Reminisce about the miracles He has done for you. Thank Him daily for nourishing food, plentiful clothes, a warm bed, good friends, health and peace. Remember, "Every good and perfect gift is from above . . ." (James 1:17) Keep the Lord a very real part of your daily lives.

THE SILENT LISTENER

In growing up, I was reminded at every meal by a framed picture which hung over our table:

> Christ is the Head of this house,
> The Unseen Guest at every meal,
> The Silent Listener to each conversation.

Please be sure that the "Silent Listener" never hears you criticize your husband or your pastor in front of your children. Both husband and pastor are symbols of God's authority in your home. If you tarnish or destroy them with biting, belittling words, you will warp your child's picture of Father God. A sweet children's song admonishes:

> Oh, be careful little mouth what you say,
> Oh, be careful little mouth what you say,
> For the Father up above is looking down in love,
> So be careful little mouth what you say.

WEAVING THE WORD INTO THEIR LIVES

Children must be trained in righteousness just as they are trained to behave or to eat the right foods or to honor authority. Our faith stands upon the Word of God. I believe six basic threads should be woven into the fabric of your child's knowledge of God's Word. Three are from the Old Testament and three from the New.

1. *The Book of Genesis* is a tapestry of richly colored stories about the beginning of our world, our history, and our faith. When a child has been taught from Year One that God created the world and formed mankind with His own hands, that child is not likely to be drawn downward into evolutionary theories.

2. *The Ten Commandments* are the bedrock of morality which have held civilization above the grip of chaos for thousands of years. These Ten Rules for Living are absolute, never changing, black and white eternal truths.

3. *The Twenty-third Psalm* brings comfort and promise of a caring Shepherd who will be there always to guide and protect.

4. *The Lord's Prayer* is our example of the really important parts of life that we must cover daily with prayer.

5. *John 3:16*, the most beloved verse in all Scripture, assures your child of the everlasting love of God and opens the way of eternal life to him.

6. *The Fruit of the Spirit* in Galatians 5:22, 23 show the character traits that grow in the life of a boy or girl who truly loves and lives for Jesus.

TOGETHER IN PRAYER

In addition to these six basics of the Word, we must teach our children how to communicate with God Himself. We must teach them how to pray. Remember the plaque hanging on Grandmother's wall: "The family that prays together stays together." Pray about everything, large and small. About her first tooth coming out. About how Coach rarely puts him into the game, even though he has practiced faithfully. About everything which is of concern to them.

As they reach high school, pray with them daily to stay true to Jesus, to withstand the peer pressure against Christian values. Praying should come as naturally as breathing. When he cannot remember the answer on a test, "Jesus, help me think." When the Big Man on Campus asks her to go to an upcoming beer party with all the popular crowd, "Oh, Lord, help me say No, even though I'd love to be seen with this guy."

Righteousness must never be equated with a long list of religious do's and don't's. Rather, it is seeking to please Jesus instead of ourselves. To train your child in righteousness give him this guiding principle: In every questionable situation ask yourself, "What would Jesus do?" That will settle the issue for him. Perhaps in your family time, you could share the great Christian classic "In His Steps" by Charles Sheldon which is based on this same premise, "What would Jesus do?"

SEEING GOD'S HAND AT WORK

Our own example must serve as their model. If Kip had never seen me seeking for answers in God's Word, how would he have known to turn there for himself? When he heard us cry out to God for solutions to impending failures, he recognized the hand of God at work as he saw those knotty problems untangle before our eyes.

When we moved to Dallas, Kip enrolled in a large public school known for its award-winning band. The school from which he had come provided all instruments for the band members, including the trumpet Kip had used. In his new school, each child was responsible to buy his own instrument. Our move to the city had exhausted all our available funds. There was simply no money for a trumpet. Kip had $75.00 from closing out his savings account when we moved. So, we prayed. "Lord Jesus, You sent us here to Dallas. Now Kip needs a trumpet. He only has $75.00, so somewhere in this city You must have someone who will sell him a horn for that price. Lord, lead us to that person quickly please, because Kip needs the trumpet now. Thank You for providing what he needs. In Jesus' Name, Amen."

I picked up a "Bargain Post" paper at the grocery store and scanned the Musical Instruments section. There it was: "Trumpet–$75.00". Robert immediately called and took Kip over that very afternoon. The ad had been placed by a professional musician who simply had collected too many horns over the years. He was selling all except the ones he used. This man took a real interest in Kip, showed him several playing techniques, and sold him a beautiful, gleaming silver-plated Besson trumpet, complete with black leather case, extra mouthpiece, and valve oil for $75.00! Truly, God is faithful.

SHARING OUR STORIES OF FAITH

"The living, the living—they praise you, as I am doing today: fathers tell their children about your faithfulness." (Isaiah 38:19) Now Kip has become a father. He has his trumpet story as one example to tell his children how faithful is the God we serve. "Only be careful, and watch yourselves closely so that you do not forget the things your eyes have seen or let them slip from your heart as long as you live. Teach them to your children and to their children after them." (Deuteronomy 4:9)

Take time to remember.

Holidays are marvelous occasions to recall the family blessings God has given us. The extended family and friends are gathered around. We are catching up on all the latest news from Uncle Paul and Aunt Helen. The cousins are growing up tall and lovely. The "Do you remember's?" are being smiled across the room. What a perfect time for the generations to share the kindness of the Lord.

The children listen intently to dear Charles as he recalls how he prayed for sardines in Germany during the War, because he was so hungry for sardines. Lo and behold! The Lord brought him a whole case of those little fish on a captured German army supply truck. And when the next building on the horizon turned out to be the dreaded Dachau death camp, Charles had a ready supply of protein to spoonfeed those starving, emaciated people. How amazing!

Pappaw Summers tells how as a teenage boy he was shot in the stomach in a hunting accident and almost died. But his godly mother stayed by his side, praying through the night and through the next day and on into the next until God touched him and delivered him from the very jaws of death. The children of two generations listen and fervently declare, "Wow, God is good!"

You may not have such dramatic, life-changing stories to tell of God's intervention. Yet *every* answer to prayer is important in showing God's hand of provision and protection. Take time to remember.

THREE KERNELS OF CORN

Every Thanksgiving as we gather around our bountifully laden table, we see three kernels of corn on each plate. This is to visibly remind us of how our forefathers sacrificed that first year they came to settle our land. They endured danger, disease, and heartbreak to chart a new course of freedom for us. That first harsh winter a great many of them died in their new land. Food became so scarce that the survivors counted every grain of corn as precious, life-sustaining. When harvest time came the next fall, they gathered the bounty with great thanksgiving to God. Today those three hard kernels of corn sitting on the beautiful china plate remind us of the price paid by those brave men and women. Each person around our table, from the head of the family right down to the smallest child, picks up the three grains of corn and tells three reasons why he is blessed this Thanksgiving.

As Rudyard Kipling wrote in his poem *Recessional*,

Lord God of Hosts, be with us yet,
Lest we forget, lest we forget.

Your example in righteousness will build confidence in God into your family. The same holds true for your example in finances. Let your children see you giving to the Lord. When the offering plate comes by, put in your money and tell them that we honor Jesus with our finances as well as our love.

The Stutzmans were a fine family in our congregation who had completed their missions training with Wycliffe Bible Translators. They were bound for Papua/New Guinea. Usually we send our missionaries out with a generous cash offering, but this time the Lord clearly impressed me to do something different. On their final Sunday with us, we honored them with love, prayer, and the gift from our congregation of a battery-powered Yamaha keyboard. Bob and Verna received the gift with joyous amazement. Their young son Jason was absolutely thunderstruck. He grabbed that keyboard, clutching it tightly to his heart while his face shone like an angel. It happened to be Mother's Day, and Verna unfolded a marvelous Mother's Day miracle for us:

"You cannot know how much this means to us," she said. "We have longed to have a keyboard like this to take overseas with us and teach songs out in the bush. Jason has been trying to learn how to play, but we could never afford lessons for him, much less a piano. In fact, for the past few weeks I had been saving all the quarters we could spare hoping to give Jason a birthday party at the pizza place. But when his birthday came, there simply wasn't enough money."

By this time the entire congregation was fixed in rapt attention, listening with ears and hearts.

The young mother continued. "We prayed about what to do with the small amount of money I had saved. Jason decided, Mom, let's give it to Robin to help on her missions trip." (Robin was a young lady in our church going to Germany for a summer of service.) "So we sealed up the quarters in an envelope labeled 'For Robin's Trip' and last Sunday Jason gave his birthday money to the Lord." Tears welled in her eyes as she smiled at her ten-year-old son cuddling the keyboard. She simply concluded, "Now this. Thank you for giving God's gift to us."

Our Lord has such a marvelous sense of timing. And there was more to come. A young man in our church family was so touched by this child's sacrifice that he immediately came to Bob and Verna at the conclusion of the service. "You bring Jason and all the friends he wants to come with him to Mr. Jim's Pizza Place before you leave town. My treat. Any time."

Not only had Verna taught Jason to pray and to give, she had also taught him to care for others with an unselfish love. She had already built God's principles into Jason's young life.

WHOLE AND HAPPY FAMILIES

It is so important that Instruction in Righteousness be done in a spirit of joy. Children need to know that God loves them so much He wants them to be *happy*. "Serve the Lord with gladness; come before his presence with singing." (Psalm 100:2 KJV) Involve your family faithfully in a good church body where you can look forward to going to the house of worship each Sunday. "I rejoiced with those who said to me, Let us go to the house of the Lord." (Psalm 122:1)

I will leave with you a simple acrostic for a happy family. It is built around the word L-O-V-E, the basis for all good things.

L: Laughter and lovely fun times. Knit your hearts together.
O: Openness must be ongoing. Keep the channels of communication clear.
V: Vision is vital. Show them Jesus in your life and your words.
E: Encouragement to excellence. Speak life and hope to them.
God loves families. He loves your family. He wants your

children to be whole and happy. Rest in that assurance and trust in His promise: "And all thy children shall be taught of the Lord; and great shall be the peace of thy children." (Isaiah 54:13 KJV)

CHAPTER
5

*SEE NO EVIL,
HEAR NO EVIL,
SPEAK NO EVIL*

"to be discreet"
Titus 2:5

D o you remember those funny little mottos and curios? They hung on Grandmother's walls. They perched on her whatnot shelves. They were stitched into her sofa pillows. Sometimes they were tacky, sometimes tender. But they were part of the decor of almost every home we knew as children. We have discarded them over the years as our tastes have grown more "sophisticated." But their messages are imbedded in our memories, as much a part of our growing up years as bicycles and braces.

Remember your grandmother's bedroom? Can you still see that picture of the beautiful Guardian Angel guiding the children over the old rickety bridge across the chasm? What a comforting image to hold in your mind until you dropped into Dreamland.

In the dining room you can probably recall some replica of the Last Supper. That was a big favorite of those days. The overworked masterpiece found itself imprinted on every medium from framed prints to three-dimensional plastic to carved soapstone. There they were, ever before you, Jesus telling His disciples, "Do this in remembrance of me."

A LESSON FROM THREE MONKEYS

One inimitable objet-d'art meant to amuse as well as moralize was the Three Little Monkeys piece. Remember that one? Three monkeys perched side by side. The first covered his eyes with tiny paws, the next one covered his ears, while the third held his paws over his mouth. The lesson they offered was "See no evil, hear no evil, speak no evil." They were the soul of discretion.

In our modern world of "Sees all! Hears all! Tells all!" we could take a lesson from those three monkeys. Particularly in today's press, the guideline seems to be no holds barred, every detail bared. Magazines blare headlines of any celebrity's most intimate life. If one is famous, he is fair game for them. Have you heard some of the radio talkshows lately? Since the callers are anonymous they feel free to spout the most vitriolic opinions, carping and criticizing. Self-styled experts dispense advice on every subject imaginable, from your personal sex problems, to your children's failures, to your parents' hangups.

Talk, talk, talk. No wonder talk is cheap. We are flooded with it. Most people begin their days with "Good Morning, America" or one of the other morning newstalk shows on television. Many end their waking hours with late night talk shows. Talk, talk, talk.

In the midst of this "Let it all hang out" generation, we are directed as women of God to be discreet.

To be discreet? Who is teaching on discretion these days? What does it mean–to be discreet?

Consider:

A discreet woman is careful to say the wise thing and to behave the right way, especially in ticklish or touchy situations.

A discreet woman will hold a confidence in spite of repeated pressure from others to tell what she knows.

A discreet woman is wise and watchful, pondering things in her heart instead of proclaiming them with her mouth.

A discreet woman is tactful in dealing with others, especially her family and friends.

124

A discreet woman knows when *not* to listen, thus immediately excusing herself from the conversation.

HOLDING BACK THE BUBBLES

Perhaps the reason God put this specific directive to women in His Word is because He knows that most women like to talk. We are emotional beings, and emotions tend to bubble over into words. When something happens, we just have to *tell* somebody! But this is the time to be careful, to be discreet. To pay attention to what we are saying, not just babble on and on.

We must begin to realize how very powerful words are. Our entire universe was called into creation by God's words. "And God said . . . and God called . . ." (Genesis 1:3,5) Jesus Himself is "the Word." (John 1:1) There is power in the words we speak, power to create or to destroy. "The tongue has the power of life and death." (Proverbs 18:21) Therefore, we must be aware of what we are saying when we speak. We must consider our words carefully.

A discreet woman will not tell everything she knows to everyone she meets. When you have a problem, only those people who can be part of the solution need to know about it. How often have you shared your heart with someone who did no more than cluck sympathetically? You later wished she didn't know so much about your personal life. Then you found yourself putting distance between the two of you because you had been indiscreet. Do not let your emotions betray you into pouring intimate thoughts into an untrustworthy ear. More friendships have been ruined by too many words than by too few. We all need those special friends who have proven themselves worthy of our confidence. They should be cherished, never overloaded. When you call a dear friend to dump your troubles on her, be sure to thank her and pray together. To be sure, most of our problems would be resolved if we spent half the time on our knees that we spend talking on the telephone.

WOUNDING WORDS OF A TALEBEARER

The fewer people you confide in, the less likely you are to hear your heartbreak floating on the wind. One of life's bitter disappointments is finding that someone you trust has broken your confidence. It feels like a betrayal, although it may have happened quite innocently. This was one of my painful, never-to-be-forgotten lessons:

A couple I'll call Chuck and Karen was passing through some turbulent marital waters. In this case, the wife was handling her emotions far better than the husband. Because of his woebegone countenance, everybody around them knew something was wrong. When people asked me, I always replied, "Just pray for them."

One morning as we were entertaining friends who had been overseas in ministry, we heard the doorbell ring. At our front door stood an overwrought Chuck. He had just ended a dreadful scene with Karen, and he was ready to fold up the marriage. Of course Robert excused himself to tend to this hurting man, and I was left to face two startled friends. Finally they asked, "What in the world is wrong with Chuck? When we left, everything was fine."

Because I trusted this couple, because they were in ministry, and probably because I was so tired of covering this problem which had dragged on for months, I told them more than "Just pray." Not the details, of course, nor the private, personal parts, but still more than I should have said. Yet these were two godly, trustworthy people who knew Chuck and Karen and cared about them. So we prayed together about this painful situation.

A week or so later as our friends talked with another couple, their discussion turned to how many people were having marital problems. Needless to say, Chuck and Karen's names were mentioned. The wife, who had known Karen a long time, was horrified. She promptly called Karen to have her explain the whole situation in order to "stop the gossip" that was going on about them. So Karen cried and told Chuck. And the next stop for a furious Chuck was at our doorstep.

As you can imagine, the few things I had shared were greatly inflated and twisted by the time I was confronted with my indiscretion.

It took many apologies and much repentance to put things to rights. Everyone involved learned a great deal about keeping our mouths shut. Chuck learned the consequences of showing up unannounced at our door every time he had a crisis. I learned never to say more than "Just pray" even with people I believe I can trust. The couple I shared with learned "Whoever repeats the matter separates close friends." (Proverbs 17:9) When they heard the results of their own indiscretion they were devastated. And the wife who called Karen learned that she was not as close a friend as she had thought, for she did not *solve* anything. She only stirred more trouble for everyone. We all lost something because we were not discreet.

Twice the Word specifically warns, "The words of a talebearer are as wounds, and they go down into the innermost parts of the belly." (Proverbs 18:8 and 26:22 KJV)

This clever warning sign was posted everywhere during World War II:

LOOSE LIPS
SINK SHIPS

It was a constant reminder that the enemy could be anywhere lurking, listening, ready to destroy. Truly that is a picture of our lives. Our enemy is ready to take anything we say and use it against us to separate, to divide, to hurt. We must be careful to speak no evil. Every morning we must pray Psalm 19:14, "Let the words of my mouth and the meditation of my heart be acceptable in thy sight, O Lord, my strength and my redeemer." (KJV)

BRAKES FOR THE RUNAWAY TONGUE

If your mouth always runs away with you, please realize you need the Lord's strength to put divine brakes on a runaway tongue.

When I say a discreet woman will not tell everything she knows to everyone she meets, I am specifically including our own personal history. How many times have you heard a variation of this theme:

"Guess what? I'm finally pregnant!"

"Well, good luck. I hope you have an easier time than I did. I went into false labor twice and the doctor was talking Caesarian section and blah, blah, blah . . ."

The joyous expression on her face changes to an anxious frown. Negative talk has just leached the happiness out of her long-awaited announcement.

Why do that? Why not let her revel in her good news? She does not need to hear every difficult pregnancy story we know. We can extinguish the light of happiness so quickly with thoughtless words. Words that put *us* and *our* problems at centerstage. Bite your tongue. Zip your lips. Whatever it takes.

SOUR WORDS SPOIL THE PUNCH

By nature I am a party-giver. I enjoy planning special events for special people. Several times I have served a delicious banana-based fruit punch. At one party I actually had people standing over the punchbowl because they couldn't get enough. That recipe was a real winner.

Then I served it at Muriel's shower. This party was going so well. Muriel was basking in the love and generosity of her friends. They were enjoying the unique entertainment. It was lovely. Until I served the refreshments.

A woman I'll call Sylvia picked up her punch cup, sipped, and stopped short, eyes wide. "Oh, no! Does this punch have bananas in it?" she demanded.

"Well, yes, it does," I replied.

"Ohmigosh, I can't drink this stuff. No, no, no. I'm violently allergic to bananas. The last time I ate something that had a banana in it—I think it was fruit salad—I threw up right there at the table."

Suddenly I noticed my other guests begin to look questioningly at their punch, as if somehow this wonderful concoction had been transformed into a cup of doom. Although the rest of the party was a success, for me it was marred forever by Sylvia's ungracious, blunt pronouncement.

The discreet thing would have been to slip quietly into the kitchen, pour the offensive beverage down the drain, and get a cup of water. Then no one would have been subjected to the crude mental image of Sylvia vomiting while they were munching their party fare.

Do you know anyone like Sylvia? There are people who seem to relish bringing up gory subjects at the dinnertable. Please, please bring discretion to the table with you. Mealtimes ought to be as pleasant as possible.

No arguments allowed.

No whining or complaining or nagging.

No bathroom subjects discussed.

No hospital scenarios nor "blood and guts" stories recounted. Perhaps you do not have a weak stomach, but have mercy on those of us who do.

A PACEMAKER AND A PEACE MAKER

I remember one dinner conversation in which an older lady began describing how a pacemaker works, how it is inserted into the body, how the skin is peeled back—you get the picture. So did I! So vivid was my mental image that five minutes of this had my stomach churning. I flashed a wireless "Help!" at my hostess who was obviously distressed to watch her guests turning green. When the older woman paused for breath, Elizabeth jumped in with a change of subject. However, this woman was fully launched on her own train of thought. She took it right up again, much to our dismay. Finally our hostess gently said, "Please, let's discuss something more pleasant while we're eating," and proceeded into another channel of thought.

So you see, being discreet extends not only to our own words, but to handling the words of others as well. A discreet woman will learn to handle potentially embarrassing situations with great tact. Otherwise the results can be damaging to everyone involved.

As guests at a banquet to honor a great man of God, Robert and I were seated at a round table with three other couples. This was a festive occasion. The city lights glittered far below the penthouse club. We were all dressed in our finery. The conversation sparkled with wit and repartee.

As we discussed who had been skiing in Colorado that season, one of the men remarked, "We considered renting a condom up there, but decided against it." Conversation paused. Eyes blinked. Obviously the man meant "condominium." But that was *not* what he said. Do we laugh? Do we point out his mistake and make him feel like a fool? Do we accuse him of a Freudian slip? Such responses are exactly what most people today would do. In fact, a comedian could sketch a whole routine with that one slip of the tongue.

Kindness and discretion prevailed. Immediately another guest stepped in with, "Not to change the subject, but have you noticed how lovely Mary looks tonight?" Mary was the wife of our guest of honor. Attention was diverted to her in a most positive way. The course of conversation flowed a different direction, and the whole table breathed an almost audible sigh of relief. The precarious moment passed. I doubt that the man ever even realized what a gaffe he had committed—until his wife got him home.

GRACIOUS CORRECTION

Most of us have enough problems with our self-esteem without having to endure ridicule when we make mistakes. A discreet woman will tactfully cover others, thereby preserving the dignity of everyone.

What if it is an obvious mistake that must be corrected such as someone giving the wrong directions? Or the wrong date? The main thing to remember about correction is that it must be given lovingly. "Speaking the truth in love" is what we are instructed to do. (Ephesians 4:15 KJV) In offering correction, a person can come across as a supercilious know-it-all: "You dummy, I've told you ten times that the meeting's on Friday, and you *still* got it wrong." Or it can be done in a gracious way: "I believe we need to coordinate our calendars. I had written down Friday the 17th as the date for that meeting." The second option leaves room for the mistaken one to save face. However, there are a great many people who feel the need to prove their own rightness by correcting others publicly.

What about correcting someone's behavior, as Karen's friend wanted to do? You can only correct one whom you have served. If a person knows you love her because of all your past dealings with her, only then can you correct her in love. Many times people see error and immediately wade in "where angels fear to tread." They only bring harm or humiliation or rebellion to an already tense situation because they have no right to meddle in that person's life.

Remember, a discreet woman is wise and watchful, pondering things in her heart, praying about them rather than talking. There is "a time to be silent and a time to speak." (Ecclesiastes 3:7) If you see error or danger in another's life, take it first to the Lord. Prayer is a mighty force for changing things. God may make you an intercessor for that one you are concerned about. Perhaps no one else is praying for her. If after much time with the Lord about the matter you still feel you need to sound a warning, go in all meekness and humility. Harsh criticism rarely brings positive results. It usually throws up barriers of self-defense. Remember, only God knows a person's heart. Let your words bring healing and wholeness.

HEARING BEYOND THE WORDS

Have you ever considered what your words tell other people

about the real you? I can easily discern what is most important to you. All I need do is listen to what you talk about most. "Out of the overflow of the heart the mouth speaks." (Matthew 12:34) "For where your treasure is, there your heart will be also." (Matthew 6:21) Your heart will be filled with what you value most, and your mouth will speak of those things. It is fascinating to listen. A discreet woman knows how to hear beyond what is being said.

Sharon spends 90% of her words talking about her children, their triumphs and tragedies.

Martha spends 90% of her time moaning about her unhappy marriage.

Donna discusses at length how expensive her clothes are, how much she is spending on redecorating the house, how much her husband's next business deal will likely make.

Ann almost always talks about the goodness of the Lord and what new thing He is doing in her life.

Sharon's treasure is her children. Martha's heart is filled with fear of failure. Donna's treasure is self-importance. Ann's heart flows out honey on all those around her. Guess who I would rather spend my time with.

A GENTLE AND QUIET SPIRIT

When we cultivate a gentle and quiet spirit, which by the way is of great value in God's eyes (I Peter 3:4), we will overcome a major source of conversational irritation: interruptions. Does it bother you when someone consistently breaks right into the middle of your sentence? Of course it does. We will not tolerate such behavior from our children yet we often find ourselves doing exactly the same thing.

Much analyzing has been done about the person who interrupts. Some say it denotes a powerplay from a forceful person who wants to control what is being said. Others say it shows an excitable person who cannot control her emotions or contain herself. Still others claim that insecurity makes one overcompensate and thus try to dominate the conversation.

I say it is downright rude, and we need to stop it. Yes, I know there are some people who rattle on forever (it seems) without even pausing for breath. In such cases we might be forgiven for trying to stem the deluge of words. But in general, common courtesy should allow the other person time to complete her thought. A discreet woman is always courteous.

Then there are those women who are always "popping off." Giving someone a piece of their mind. "Well, I'll just tell you what I think." Most times they have not given any thought at all to what they are about to express. They just react, "pop off." They can tell you in two minutes precisely how they would resolve racial tensions or dry up the drug problems or tackle the terrorists. No one takes them seriously though, because their simplistic solutions show they have no grasp of these complex situations. They use no wisdom nor discretion.

ONLY JOKING?

Another conversational device a discreet woman will avoid is what I call "innocent teasing." This is when a person needles you with so much sugarcoating on her words that you are never quite sure if you have been stabbed. You usually have been. You can tell because your heart is sore.

One of my earliest memories is of a beloved family member teasing me, picking at me until I cried. Then he called me a "crybaby" because, after all, he didn't mean any harm. He was just teasing me. So why did it hurt so much? This hurtful, playful teasing is in the same category as unbearable tickling. Both start out as affection, but end up in pain.

If you wonder whether someone is saying something in an oblique way with her teasing, the answer is Yes. If she did not think it, she would not have it in her heart to say, even teasingly. She is covering herself though so if you confront her she can always back down by saying, "Oh, I was just teasing. Can't you take a little joke?"

"Like a madman shooting firebrands or deadly arrows is a man who deceives his neighbor and says, I was only joking." (Proverbs 26:18,19)

Jesus gave us some very sound advice when He warned, "Simply let your Yes be Yes and your No, No; anything beyond this comes from the evil one." (Matthew 5:37) His brother James tells us that our tongue can defile everything we do. (James 3) Be discreet in what you say. It will save much grief.

Along with "popping off" and "innocent teasing" we also find the "playful putdown." Our society relishes putting people down. Celebrity roasts are favorite forms of entertainment. This is where you strip someone of her dignity and then laugh about it. You poke fun at a failure or foible, and everyone thinks you are hilarious, except the object of your ridicule.

Husbands and wives do this to one another all the time. "Alice," he will announce to the whole table, "you've got spinach hung in your teeth. I gotta tell you, Babe, it really clashes with your lipstick. Ha—ha—ha." This type of "humor" can be habit-forming. It can get such a hold on your mind that you find yourself responding this way unintentionally.

Robert and I were the speakers one summer at a lovely family camp in Upstate New York. This quiet place was nestled beside a lake in beautiful, rolling hills. Days were bright and sunny, evenings crisp and clear. The people were responding joyfully to our ministry. We were having a blessed time.

Then Skipper showed up.

SKIPPER'S STORY

One morning at lakeside I was gazing out over the still waters collecting my thoughts before I spoke. Our pastor/host brought someone over to meet me. This person was a grizzled, leathery-looking man about 60 years old. The deep seams on his face evidenced years of squinting into sun-brilliant waters. His calloused hands had handled miles of rope. His jaunty cap and jutting jaw were those of a sailor. "Jo, I want you to meet Skipper," introduced the Pastor. "He's a tugboat captain. Skipper, this is Jo. She is teaching the morning session today."

"Hello, Skipper," I smiled.

He sized me up slowly. Finally, "Jo? Jo! What kinda name is that for a pretty lady like you? Ha–ha–ha."

I was a bit taken aback. I could not decide if I had just been complimented or insulted. Trying to be gracious, I replied, "I was named after my father. His name is Jofred. Mine is JoAn."

"Well, yeah, I was named after my old man too. That's why I go by Skipper. Ain't no way I'm gonna let folks call me by that ol' buzzard's name. Ha–ha–ha."

What is this man's problem? I raised questioning eyebrows at the Pastor.

He merely smiled and said, "Skipper, be sure you come to hear Jo's teaching this morning. You'll be interested in it."

"Why? What're you gonna talk about?" he queried.

I looked him straight in the eye. "The power of the tongue," I replied.

CAUGHT IN A TANGLED NET

Sure enough, there he sat in the fourth row on the right while I taught many of the same things I am saying here. His watery blue eyes never wavered from me. Yet I could detect no response in his fixed stare.

At lunchtime there happened to be one empty chair at our table, right beside me. Can you guess who walked up and put his tray in that place? That's right: Skipper. I sent a silent plea heavenward. "Oh Lord, why does he have to sit here? I'm tired. I've ministered the

135

whole morning. Please just make him go away." No sooner had I beseeched the Lord to remove this man's presence than I turned to find a much subdued Skipper speaking to me.

"I listened to every word you said this morning, Jo, and I know it's all true. But I can't help myself. Sometimes just before I start to say somethin' hateful I'll hear a little voice tellin' me, 'Skipper, don't say it, man, don't.' But I go ahead anyhow and I always wind up makin' people mad or hurtin' their feelings." He shook his head slowly. In a tone of despair he asked, "Why do I do that?" And a big tear traced its way down his careworn cheek.

I just melted. I reached over and took his big, gnarled hand. "Because, Skipper, you are caught in a net of your own making, a tough net woven by years of harsh responses and hard life." He nodded his head thoughtfully, as if gazing down the pain-filled years he had lived through. I called him back. "But Skipper, you don't have to live this way, all tangled up. Jesus said He came to set the captives free, to set *you* free." Hope began to flicker in his brimming eyes. I pressed on, "Right now, this very minute, the loving power of Jesus Christ can set you free. You just have to ask."

By this time, of course, the whole table was listening, longing to help. I could sense silent prayers interceding for a hardened tugboat captain. We were about to witness a miracle.

CLEAN HEART, CLEAN TONGUE

"I—I—don't know how to ask," he faltered.

"Then Robert will lead the way for you," I said. "Just follow his prayer and mean it with all your heart."

Robert took over from there, leading Skipper in a beautiful prayer of deliverance from evil. The tears flowed, washing away years of bitterness and pain. It was a precious moment when Skipper looked up and said wonderingly, "I feel clean!"

That is what the blood of Jesus does for us. "For you know

that it was not with perishable things such as silver or gold that you were redeemed from the empty way of life handed down to you from your forefathers, but with the precious blood of Christ, a lamb without blemish or defect." (I Peter 1:18,19)

If your life has been filled with pain or negativity or bitterness as Skipper's had, then your tongue will speak like that until the love of Jesus cleanses you, makes you whole again, and delivers your tongue from evil. "Whoever would love life and see good days must keep his tongue from evil and his lips from deceitful speech." (I Peter 3:10)

How sobering it is to realize that someday each of us will stand before God Almighty to give account for every idle, useless word we have spoken in our life. (Matthew 12:36) All the popping off, all the gossip, all the putdowns, all the foolish jesting—how will we explain all that? Jesus said, "By thy words thou shalt be justified, and by thy words thou shalt be condemned." (Matthew 12:37 KJV) Much, much better it is for us to confess these idle words as sin, ask for forgiveness, and bury them in the sea of forgetfulness, never to repeat them again.

A MOUTH THAT NEVER STOPPED

A bright, witty young man I'll call Mick worked with Robert and me on several different creative projects. He was clever and gifted, but Mick also had a mouth that never stopped. He spouted opinions, jokes, gossip, and criticism (though never malicious) about every topic that crossed his path. Sometimes he bordered on the sacrilegious. Yes, he was funny. Yes, he would say almost anything for a laugh. I cannot count the times I remonstrated, "Mick, when you get to Heaven you will probably spend your first 100 years in a deprogramming chamber giving account for all the foolish jesting and idle words you utter!" But Mick was master of the snappy comeback, and I never did make him realize the gravity of his runaway mouth.

Paul the Apostle put foolish talking and jesting into the same category with obscenity. "Nor should there be obscenity, foolish talk or coarse joking, which are out of place. . ." (Ephesians 5:4) That should give us pause. Let's begin to hear our words as the Lord hears them.

THE TONE OF OUR VOICE

Have you ever heard your voice on a tape player and said, "That doesn't sound like me!" You ought to leave the tape recorder on all day long. You might be astounded at what it captures. So often we do not realize what the tone of our voice says.

Marsha's voice always sounds whiny. Mary's voice lifts my spirits because it is always so positive. Sue's voice conveys disapproval in almost every conversation. How does your voice sound most of the time?

A young mother told me recently, "When I heard Annie in her room roundly scolding her dolls, I pulled myself up short. I heard her using my own tone of voice, and I did *not* like what I heard."

It puzzles me why many people are more pleasant to strangers than to their own families. Are you as gracious in explaining math to your son as you are in giving directions to a passerby? Are you charming on the telephone and grumpy as soon as you hang up? Do you respect your boss's decisions, but always question your husband's? The answers can be discerned simply by the tone of your voice.

"Let your conversation be always full of grace, seasoned with salt, so that you may know how to answer everyone." (Colossians 4:6) Grace and discretion are watchwords for every conversation.

As a child, I often listened to my favorite record album from the movie "Bambi." I could recite the whole soundtrack by memory. I can still hear the exchange between Thumper and his mother as they watched little Bambi trying to learn to walk.

"He doesn't walk very good, does he?" Thumper pointedly observed.

"Thumper!"

"Yes, Mama?"

"What did your father tell you this morning?"

Much subdued, "If ya can't say somethin' nice, don't say nuthin' at all."

That sage bit of wisdom I learned as a child has held true throughout my lifetime.

Being discreet certainly applies to our behavior as well as our words. I have placed the major emphasis of this chapter on the tongue, for that is where most of our troubles begin. After all, "If anyone is never at fault in what he says, he is a perfect man, able to keep his whole body in check." (James 3:2)

Discretion in our behavior is a simple matter of conducting ourselves with propriety. In others words, we behave in such a godly way that we do not leave ourselves open to questionable criticism. We simply do what is proper for one who calls herself by Christ's Name. We abstain from all appearance of evil. (I Thessalonians 5:22)

One of the Summers household rules was that our son Kip never brought his girlfriend home alone when we were gone. We trusted our son implicitly. He was a godly young man, and he always dated Christian girls. So why this household rule? To protect their pure reputations. To prevent unnecessary temptations. To provide examples of restraint for other young people. To abstain from any appearance of evil.

Robert does not counsel a hurting woman alone in his office. Either I am there with him or another staff member is available to him. Why? So that there is no opportunity for a sense of intimacy and dependency to develop on the part of one who needs a strong man to lean on. It is tragic to realize how many ministers have fallen prey to the enemy when they simply started out to help someone in distress.

CAUGHT IN THE TRAP

A handsome young minister I'll call Samson (because he thought he was really strong) was appointed to the visitation ministry at his church. He was to comfort the afflicted and bring hope to the despairing ones. The Senior Pastor specifically told Sam he could not take his wife along on this visitation ministry because she might slow him down. They would stop to shop or linger over lunch if she were along, he reasoned. That would be considered bad stewardship of the time and money the church was investing in Sam. (What incredibly poor judgment!)

You can guess what happened, of course. The enemy set up a classic situation with a divorced Delilah. This lovely blonde woman needed much counseling from her handsome pastor. He could help heal the hurts of her broken marriages. He could bring some release from the humiliations of her sordid sexual past as she shared the intimate details with him—alone. Wham! The trap slammed shut. Sam was caught in an emotional tangle with a woman who was determined to have him. His bewildered wife began to receive mysterious phone calls to alert her to her husband's comings and goings. She was devastated, yet disbelieving, for she really trusted her husband. But when the call came from the "abortion clinic" requesting payment from Samson for Delilah's abortion, this little wife caved in. Listen, the devil does not play fair. He uses every dirty trick he can think of to bring God's people to ruin.

Finally Sam went to the Senior Pastor for help. He confessed what a trap he had walked into. To his utter amazement, he was cut off without a dime. Removed from the staff immediately. Not even allowed to attend one more service to bid farewell to the people he had served for two years. Would you say he received real Christian compassion from his "Pastor" who set him up for such a fall in the first place? Hardly.

Robert and I picked up the shattered pieces of that family. With God's gracious restoring power at work, Sam and his wife were able to forgive and survive. We devoutly hope that the next time someone tries to get him in a compromising situation, he will flee for his life, as Joseph did long ago, saying, "How could I do such a thing and sin against God?" (Genesis 39:9)

UNDER THE GUISE OF FELLOWSHIP

You may think me old-fashioned or straightlaced, but I see far too much moral laxity among Christians today. I have to deal with the damage it does. Things go on under the guise of fellowship which give an open door to the enemy. Such as:
• bikini swim parties, where good friends, male and female, rub suntan oil on each other's tanned bodies;
• several couples relaxing together in a hot tub on a regular basis;
• a married man and a married woman working together on lengthy projects without either of their spouses being involved;
• lingering face-to-face "brotherly and sisterly" hugs;
• women who wear revealing or seductive clothes, pretending wide-eyed innocence;
• men who always want to pray for women, especially laying hands on them.

This list could go on and on. I could give you explicit examples of harm that came from each scenario. But you are getting the idea by now. Any one of these situations simply is not proper. We must not give any leverage to the devil, any wedge to split our homes, any way for the destroyer to seek us out for the kill.

PURITY IN A POLLUTED WORLD

Our Lord Jesus is coming for a *pure* bride. Do we understand that, Church? Purity is what He desires of us. "Beloved, now are we the sons of God, and it doth not yet appear what we shall be: but we know that, when he shall appear, we shall be like him; for we shall see him as he is. And every man that hath this hope in him purifieth himself, even as he is pure." (I John 3:2,3 KJV)

We must purify ourselves daily as we walk through a wicked world. We are surrounded constantly on every side by images of sexual sin and lurid lust. These images scream at us from billboards. They

141

invade our homes through television. They pound at our ears through the world's music. Sin is presented as desirable, as fun, as friendly. Never shown is the devastation sin really brings. "Sin, when it is finished, bringeth forth death." (James 1:15 KJV)

In ministry and counseling, I get to hear all about the deadly side of sin. Heartsick, I watch the fall of yet another godly man to immorality. I hear the tales of disbelief and betrayal. I dry the tears of the wounded, the griefstricken. My heart aches for bewildered, confused little children whose families have just been shattered. And I vow again and again, "Straightlaced or not, I will keep pushing purity."

Be discreet. Be aware. Shun the very appearance of wrong. "Discretion will protect you, and understanding will guard you." (Proverbs 2:11)

Finally, lest you remain unconvinced of the importance of discretion in your life, let me appeal to your self image through the wise words of Solomon in Proverbs 11:22, "Like a gold ring in a pig's snout is a beautiful woman who shows no discretion."

Enough said?

CHAPTER 6

FIDELITY IS FUN

In our sex-saturated society, it seems more women want to be "chased" than to be chaste. Isn't this true? Glance at the glossy covers on any magazine rack. You will see titles blaring advice on how to get that man you want, even if he is already married to somebody else. "The Subtle Art of Seduction." "How To Live Your Fantasy." "Leaving Your Guilt Behind."

When was the last time you saw a title like "Why Chastity Works"?

Chastity? The very word conjures up pictures of prim old maids with haughty eyebrows and pinched mouths. Of course. The enemy of life always uses today's media to skew public opinion away from truth toward modern morality. In fact, only the dire threat of contracting AIDS has slowed down the rampant promiscuity of this generation.

Purity, fidelity, and chastity are not portrayed as desirable virtues. Rather, they are relegated to the Plain Jane who can't get a date until she loosens up. Today's generation seems to think purity is passe;

fidelity is part of the Marine Corps slogan; and chastity is one of those obsolete words found only in the dictionary, not in modern usage. Nothing could be further from the truth!

WHAT CHASTITY REALLY MEANS

When you are married, being chaste means pure sex, God-ordained passion, fun without guilt, and the security of a lifetime partner. Chastity means purity of thought and deed.

It means being virtuous. "Who can find a virtuous woman? for her price is far above rubies." Why is a woman of virtue so rare, so priceless? Because "the heart of her husband doth safely trust in her, so that he shall have no need of spoil. She will do him good and not evil all the days of her life." (Proverbs 31:10,11,12 KJV)

A virtuous wife will be true to her husband always. He will never have any reason to doubt her faithfulness to him. She will fulfill his sexual needs by continuing to be his love covering throughout their marriage. She will not be a prude. She will try to please him more in the bedroom than she does in the kitchen. I can almost hear you saying, "I can't believe she's putting a chapter on sex right here in the middle of this book!" Why not? More marriages start coming apart in the bedroom than in any other room in the house. This ought *not* to be.

SEX FROM GOD'S PERSPECTIVE

Christian women should be the best lovers of all. We have the love of Jesus Christ flowing through our spirits, souls, and bodies. God the Father created us as sexual beings. He knew what He was doing when He put this basic urge within our bodies. Therefore, we need to develop a healthy attitude toward sex. Let's learn to see things from God's perspective, not from our cultural conditioning.

Some of you will be like Jennifer. One day she asked what

chapter I was working on. I told her I was trying to cover the broad scope of good sex in marriage. Her face lit up with a happy smile. "Oh goodie," she said, "you know that'll be the very first part most of us read." I have since learned that this young wife was struggling to understand and adjust the intimate part of her marriage. Yet she was unable even to mention her problem.

Please let this chapter be a help, a blessing to you. If talking about your intimate life embarrasses you or makes you want to run hide, than you *need* this chapter. Why is it so difficult to acknowledge that we need help in this vital area?

All of us need an older, godly woman in our lives to give us wise counsel. We should get our advice from one who has a happy marriage, not from a "misery loves company" companion.

Generally, I only hear about the problems after the husband has already walked out or given up. It always amazes me to see just how much a wife can change, out of sheer desperation, when she is about to lose her man. She can shed those thirty pounds after all. She can suddenly find time to go play with him. She can update her lingerie wardrobe. She can learn to rekindle the flame of passion that is flickering, failing. Amazing. The old saying goes, "You never miss the water 'til the well runs dry." The time to learn to please your husband is before the wellspring of his love for you runs dry.

SEX IN MARRIAGE IS WONDERFUL

I realize I am dealing with two very disparate groups of women when discussing attitudes about sex. For those of us who grew up before the so-called sexual revolution, keeping our virginity was of primary importance. Each of us wanted to wear a white dress at our wedding. In the other group are those of you who grew into sexual awareness during the New Morality (really just the Old Immorality). For many of you, virginity came to be an embarrassing burden to bear, and even brides who were four months pregnant wore white wedding

147

gowns to the altar.

As a blossoming young woman who finally reached the dating age, were you sternly warned against "giving in to the only thing boys are after?" Were you admonished by a worried mother to keep your ankles crossed and your knees together? How often did you hear, "No decent man wants damaged goods"? Or, "Boys sleep with bad girls, but they only marry good girls." As Christian teenagers we were to put our passions into a straightjacket until our wedding night. After we finally got that ring on our finger we would be free! We could throw off all restraint. Only, for most of us it was not that easy. After a young lifetime of caution, our minds said, "Good girls don't enjoy sex." Great internal struggles ensued for many of us as we tried to make love without guilt.

AT THE OTHER EXTREME

Beverly grew up with "sex is shameful" being drilled into her. She never saw open affection in her home between loving parents, because her dad had walked out when Bev was only two years old. All the hurt her mother had endured from this rejection was engraved on Beverly's soul as she heard over and over, "Boys only want your body. Don't ever get close. Don't ever give in. They'll get what they want, then they will leave you." Do you wonder that Beverly finally rebelled and got pregnant when she was only sixteen? Is it any wonder that she is now on her third marriage? May God help that beautiful woman overcome the rigid scars of her past.

How different her life could have been had she been taught the truth: Sex is wonderful when you are married! It brings joy worth waiting for, fusing your very being with that one special lifetime partner. Pure love that brings no guilt, just happiness, can be found *only* within the commitment of marriage.

This is God's plan. We must follow our Creator's best and highest intentions for this sacred part of our lives.

148

Fidelity Is Fun

APPROACH IT SQUARELY AND BIBLICALLY

This is what we must teach our young people. God loves them so much that He wants what is best for them. God hates immorality of all kinds. He specifically denounces sex sins in His Word because they destroy the very fabric of a person's emotional life. Instead of pretending our teens have no interest in sex or trying to avoid the subject as if it does not exist, we must address it squarely and biblically. Let's teach them the value of purity, the reward for self-control before marriage.

Does this sound unrealistic in today's world? It is a world where casual sex surrounds them in their schools, their movies, their music. Discuss it with them. Young people like honesty, they despise hypocrisy. Therefore, show them the acknowledged casualties of today's casual sex. Statistics abound. But you can bring it right down to where they live.

How many pregnant girls do you know in your high school? Are these girls thrilled at how their sexlife has turned out?

How many lovesick kids do you know who tried to kill themselves when that one they were sleeping with walked out?

Do you know someone who is suffering with venereal disease, perhaps genital warts?

What about the very real possibility of AIDS?

Do you know the scars that abortion leaves on a young girl's soul?

These are all very real, pertinent questions facing our young people today. We must warn them that sex before marriage is condemned by God, is attended by guilt, has potential for pregnancy, and leaves lasting damage on the soul when that relationship dies—as it almost certainly will. But we must never, never communicate that sex itself is bad. Instead, it is a gift of God worth waiting for.

We must be completely open with our kids about this subject. They get pressured in ways we never had to handle as teens. A lovely blonde girl told me, "When I was a senior in high school, I really felt like a freak. I was the only girl in my whole group of friends who was still a virgin. It was like I was sexually stunted or something. After every date I would face their questions, 'Did you do it yet?' Finally I got a guy down the street to relieve me of my burdensome virginity just so I could feel like one of the regular girls."

I felt a deep sorrow over her confession. How sad that the purity she could have brought to her Christian marriage had been stolen as she caved in to peer pressure.

Another precious friend of mine knows firsthand the lifetime sadness of unwanted teenage pregnancy. Missy gave in to her boyfriend's continued pressure, "If you love me, show me." He got her pregnant when she was only sixteen, far too young to cope with the guilt, the shame, the betrayal of her parents. Too young to keep her child, too unskilled to support a baby, she faced nine months of nurturing life within her knowing that this bond would be severed forever at birth. She signed her baby over for adoption without ever seeing his sweet face. As the years have passed, the Lord has graciously healed Missy's deep hurt from that painful time. He has restored her soul. She now has a loving husband, a darling son, and a beautiful daughter. God's grace is so marvelous.

And yet, and yet. Every year on one certain day, there is a birthday she can never celebrate except in her heart.

THE TWO LETTER WORD

When I related Missy's story to an assembly of high school girls, I told them, "Listen to me, the best birth control plan in the world is one that will work all the time, is simple to use, and doesn't cost you a dime. It is simply the two-letter word NO." Those girls clapped and cheered. "Furthermore," I continued, "when he says 'If you love me like I love you, you'll hop into bed with me' then you better know he's lying. If he *really* loves you, he'll want what is best for you. That means backing off the pressure and letting you keep your self-dignity." They stomped their feet and cheered some more.

We must give our teens such stability that they will have a secure sense of self which will not buckle under intense peer pressure. We know that the tendency to teenage promiscuity is most often rooted in parental attitudes of either extreme laxity or total rigidity.

Under extreme laxity, young people are given no spiritual anchor to hold them firmly and no consistent discipline as they develop. Therefore, they do not feel loved. They think their behavior, sexual or otherwise, is of no importance to their parents. They are given too much freedom, are left to their own devices. Ultimately, most of them fulfill the scripture, "A child left to himself bringeth his mother to shame." (Proverbs 29:15 KJV)

At the other end of the spectrum we find the totally rigid, unbending parent. In this case, the child feels so stifled by overbearing rules and meaningless restrictions that he finally refuses to live under such constraint. He kicks over the traces and races headlong to self-destruction.

This very thing happened to one of my best friends. She was never allowed to date. She could not participate in school activities, for they were deemed too worldly. She could only socialize with a few church kids. Her parents' concept of God was so narrow she decided there was no way she could ever please Him or them. So she stopped trying. She looked for love wherever she could find it, and soon she was pregnant.

THROUGH THE MINEFIELDS OF TEMPTATION

Parenting a teenager is not easy even under the best of circumstances. We daily need the mind of Christ to guide our teens through the minefields of temptation set before them. We must love them, cherish them in spite of minor conflicts that arise when they begin loosening the apron strings. Many times I was spared from harm simply by thinking, "If I did this and Mother found out, it would kill her."

151

I loved my mom so much that I would turn my back on the temptation. An open, loving relationship with our teenagers is vital to their protection.

Many mothers feel they ought to find work outside the home when their children are no longer small. After all, teenagers can take care of themselves. A second salary would certainly help. College tuition looms on the horizon. And the kids are begging for their own cars.

Yes, all that is true. But consider this: An unsupervised house can become a powerful temptation for young people who are just awakening to sexual urges. Protect your teenagers. Do not set them up as prey to pushy peers who disregard your home's moral standards.

The epidemic of unwanted pregnancies in our land today is a direct result of our sexually "liberated" society. "If it feels good, do it" is the code of conduct. This attitude has permeated every area of our lifestyles. Self-indulgence is the real name of this spirit which is choking the life out of America. "There is way that seems right to a man, but in the end it leads to death." (Proverbs 14:12) "If it feels good, do it" leads straight to emotional pain, abandonment, abortions, and hollow-eyed women who have squandered the vital part of their innermost being.

Single women, do not be lured by the siren of the world's ways. Keep yourself chaste. Keep your self-dignity intact. Choose life over death.

You may be feeling a bit hopeless right now if you are reading this and thinking, "What about me? I've already blown it big time. There's no hope for me."

No situation is hopeless in Jesus Christ. He extends mercy without measure to the truly repentant one. "If we confess our sins, he is faithful and just to forgive us our sins, and to cleanse us from all unrighteousness." (I John 1:9 KJV) Before you try to build a godly marriage, be sure you are washed and cleansed of the ungodly liaisons you entered into as a single woman. Ask the Holy Spirit to go back in time to retrieve all those pieces of your inner being that you scattered around, to replace them within you so that you can be restored to wholeness. Ask God's forgiveness. Then forgive yourself—and let the past go. "Yet this I call to mind and therefore I have hope: Because of the Lord's great love we are not consumed, for his compassions never fail. They are new every morning; great is your faithfulness." (Lamentations 3:21,22,23)

Yes, God is faithful to us in every facet of our lives, including this very special area of intimacy. If you have been wounded in the past by unholy alliances, if you were sinned against as a child who was molested, you can still be washed in the blood of Jesus, healed deep down in your emotional self, and made fresh and pure again. That is God's faithfulness.

SO DIFFERENT FROM THE DREAM

Many brides waltz down the aisle toward their grooms in a rosy glow of expectations for the future. After all, they grew up on the wonderful stories where she lived happily ever after. So this picture of a charming "ever after" is only natural.

What a shock to find reality so different from the dream. He wants to make love in the morning. She thinks sex must wait until bath and bedtime. He wants to romp with her in front of a mirror. She clings to the covers. He enjoys watching her undress because it turns him on. She is so tired of his motor always running that she decides to dress in the closet. He would really be pleased if she would do a sexy little dance for him. She is flabbergasted and wonders if he went to striptease joints before they met. On and on it goes in any number of unexpected scenarios.

At the other extreme, sometimes a bride winds up wondering what is wrong. Why is her husband's passion so quickly spent? Why doesn't he want to play more? This often happens in the case where a young man was promiscuous before his marriage. He has already had so many passionate encounters that he has lost the thrill of newness his bride expects. He may reach for her less and less. She finds herself feeling abandoned, unsatisfied, unfulfilled. It this the marital bliss she has waited for?

A SIMPLE CHANGE OF ATTITUDE

What I am pointing out here is the attitudes we bring with us into marriage. Attitudes of the heart are a sum total of our past experiences, good and bad. Most bedroom problems can be resolved with a simple change of attitude. Talk to your husband about how you feel. If a bad attitude on your part is wrecking his response toward you, then talk it out. Discuss the subject gently, prayerfully, honestly. Ask the Lord to show you why you feel the way you do. Do you feel like a sex object instead a cherished partner? If so, your husband may need to adjust his approach to you. But he will never know until you tell him.

Do you need to be healed from an old hurt? "My dad walked out on Mom and me just when I needed him the most."

Do you need to be set free from bondages created by fear? "No one has ever really loved me, so sooner or later you will probably reject me too."

Do you need forgiveness from sin in order to be able to give love freely? "I hate my parents and I hate myself, and I don't trust God because He allowed it all to happen."

As a child of the living God, you are to "put off your old self which is being corrupted by its deceitful desires; to be made new in the attitude of your minds; and to put on the new self, created to be like God in true righteousness and holiness." (Ephesians 4:22-24)

THE LORD'S WAY FOR YOU

True righteousness and holiness brings God's fulfillment to marriage. Sin is what corrupts. The more you put off the old self with its emotional bumps and bruises, the more you follow the Lord's loving way for you, the more joy you will find flowing into your relationship with your husband. After all, God made marriage the pattern for His Church! Christ as bridegroom, the Church as bride. Of course He wants us to get it right, to be happy, to be blessed in our lovelife. But it must be done *His* way.

Not the world's way.

Not the "Playboy" way, nor the fantasy way.

"It is God's will that you should be holy; that you should avoid sexual immorality; that each of you should learn to control his own body in a way that is holy and honorable, not in passionate lust like the heathen who do not know God." (I Thessalonians 4:3-5)

Some Christian couples want to dabble in the world's ways of sexual gratification, thinking it will bring a measure of excitement to their marriage. One young couple rented X-rated videos to watch before they made love. "Watching other people in bed heightened our own sexual appetite for one another," they said. "After all, we did it in the privacy of our own home, so where's the harm?"

Where's the harm? Let me tell you. What this couple did was pay money to watch the act of adultery which had been performed and filmed for profit. What kind of people make these films? Would they be welcome in that young couple's bedroom? Certainly not. Yet these two had brought the spirit of lust right into their marriage by opening their lives to this evil.

"What do righteousness and wickedness have in common? Or what fellowship can light have with darkness . . . For we are the temple of the living God. As God has said: I will live with them and walk among them, and I will be their God, and they will be my people." (II Corinthians 6:14,16) How do you think this couple would feel if the Lord Jesus walked in while they were watching such filth. Ashamed? No doubt. But since He is always with us and is in us, He *is* there while we do everything, even those things we choose to think He does not see.

The Lord calls to us, "Come out from them and be

separate . . . Touch no unclean thing, and I will receive you. I will be a Father to you, and you will be my sons and daughters." (ibid., vs. 17,18) Our wonderful Father wants us to be different, special, separate from the world. He plans to give us the very best life we can know. He will bless us with fulfillment in every area.

LOVELIFE AND HOLINESS

"Since we have these promises, dear friends, let us purify ourselves from everything that contaminates body and spirit, perfecting holiness out of reverence for God." (II Corinthians 7:1)

The problem is that somehow we have never connected a fulfilling lovelife with holiness. Instead, we thought holiness meant being prudish, sterile, antiseptic. Not so! The Word instructs, "May you rejoice in the wife of your youth . . . may her breasts satisfy you always, may you ever be captivated by her love." (Proverbs 5:18,19) Does that sound like prudish behavior? I think not.

God created us as sexual beings and established marriage to be the place for fulfillment. He honors marriage. He allowed His Son's first miracle to be performed at a wedding in Cana. (See John 2:1-11.) He specifically says in Hebrews 13:4, "Marriage should be honored by all, and the marriage bed kept pure." Yes, God is concerned about what happens in our bedroom. Our sexlife is not a separate part of us somehow disconnected from holy living.

Your lovelife ought to be fun! God ordained marriage to be the expression for pure sexual passion, for fun without guilt, and for the security of a lifetime partner. So don't let lovemaking deteriorate into a boring routine. "Well, it's Friday night. Might as well get it over with." If that is your opinion of sex, you are cheating yourself of much joy. And unless you change your attitude, you may find your husband cheating in other ways.

Do you love your husband? Then be his love covering. Try to please him in this most vital area of your covenant. Learn what turns him on. Be willing to explore new ideas in lovemaking. Ask the Lord to give you creative ways to please your man. Be aware that there are wonderful Christian books available on this subject.

No, I am not going to share my personal secrets with you. My secrets are my own and Robert's. Suffice it to say I know how to make him happy, and I enjoy a happy husband. You see, pleasing him pleases me, and so we both are happy.

LOVE-FILLED MEMORIES

Time alone, just for the two of us, has been the catalyst in keeping our marriage fresh. Sometimes we go to the beach. Other times we hide away in a woodland cottage. We have dinner at a fine restaurant and flirt with each other. We continue to date, to keep romance in our busy lives. We *make time* in the ebb and flow of life to stop at these quiet islands of love and peace.

One of my happiest memories is of a week we spent wandering around France together. Having rented a car, we meandered at our own pace. Robert is a very outgoing person who often converses with strangers. However, he cannot speak French, so for six glorious days I held his undivided attention! One morning we basked in the stained-glass beauty of the Sainte Chappelle. After picnicking in the courtyard of Notre Dame Cathedral, we climbed up its hundreds of stairs amid the glorious clamor of tolling bells. We watched the sun set from the Eiffel Tower and floated down the moonlit Seine River. And every day we made lovefilled memories.

Such ideal moments do not just happen. We must set aside time for them. We plan our little honeymoons. Of course we rarely get to some exotic place like Paris. Mostly we just take a day or two here, a quiet evening there, a symphony concert to dress up for, or a walk through the woods hand in hand. Time just for us. Time when the phone cannot intrude. Away from the insistent details of "must do" things which always press. Time for the truly important part of our lives: our love and our Lord. I emphasize that this time is simply for Robert and me, just the two of us.

WISDOM IN CLOSE FRIENDSHIPS

Many marriages encounter perilous times because there is too much sharing of life with best friends. I have seen this happen far too often. Two couples become best friends. They enjoy spending time together so much that before long they are always together. In and out of one another's homes constantly. Taking trips together. Sharing intimate details of their lives as they sip drinks together in the hot tub. Excluding other friends from their tightknit circle of four, they believe these special relationships will last for eternity.

Then life intervenes with trouble or tragedy for one of the couples. Say something happens to the husband, such as illness or career problems. He begins to flounder spiritually and emotionally. His wife does not know how to handle the problem, so she turns to his best friend for help. This is done in innocence. She realizes this best friend seems so much stronger than her failing husband, so much wiser, yes, and nobler. He reaches out to comfort her in her pain. Pity is a powerful manipulative force. Suddenly this wife finds herself in the arms of her husband's best friend and discovers she *likes* it there. No, it is not right. No, they never meant it to happen. Certainly they never started out to hurt their spouses. But there it is—the disintegration of two homes and families is imminent.

This is a no-win situation. Everybody loses. The spouses feel betrayed. The children are bewildered. Tears flow unendingly. If the two sever their ungodly emotional attachment, the former friendship is still shattered, ruined. The betrayed spouses have much grief to deal with and forgiveness to work through before the marriages can ever be restored. Both couples feel alienated from the whole world. They have no other close friends to turn to since they closed themselves off with their best friends. Now that relationship has crumbled, and there is no one left to trust.

Am I saying we cannot have good friends? Of course not. Just be wise, be watchful. "Seldom set foot in your neighbor's house," counseled wise Solomon, "too much of you, and he will hate you." (Proverbs 25:17) Too much intimacy with any person other than your own lifetime partner will eventually lead to trouble.

"The wise woman builds her house, but with her own hands the foolish one tears hers down." (Proverbs 14:1) Be wise in your dealings with friends. If you realize that another woman wants to spend more time with your husband than with you, know it is time to put some distance into that relationship. You never even have to articulate it as a threat. Simply say, "Honey, we've spent so much time with the Davises lately that we have really been neglecting our other friends. Let's change that, okay?" He may be more relieved than you know. Perhaps he has been feeling the subtle pressure build. Be the wise woman who protects her home, not the unseeing, foolish one who stumbles to ruin.

CHECK YOUR SIGNALS

We have discussed protecting your husband from other women. Now let us consider how you relate to other men, such as your husband's friends or the men in your daily activities or church. Do you give out the wrong kind of signals to them? How can you tell? Take the quiz below. Answer the questions by yourself with total honesty. Easy self-justification is in quotations.

1. Do men tell you off-color or naughty jokes? Little stories that are sexually suggestive? Do they think you want to listen?

"Oh, they just treat me like one of the boys."

2. Do you like to wear low-cut necklines or unbutton your blouse to display cleavage? Do you prefer wearing clothes that show

off your body, such as bare sundresses, short shorts, bikinis? Tight sweaters with slit skirts? Or filmy, clingy fabrics over sheer lingerie?
"Yes, they make me feel feminine."

3. Do you prefer the company of men to the company of women?
"Women are so boring."

4. Do you ever fantasize what this man or that one would be like in bed?
"It's just a fantasy. Nobody knows."

5. Do you indulge in watching soap operas?
"I'm *not* hooked on them."

6. Do you like to tease men? Is flirting fun for you?
"That's just my personality."

7. Has any of your women friends ever expressed concern about your behavior toward her husband?
"She was just a jealous idiot."

8. At the beach or pool, are you happy when men notice you? Do you respond to their friendly overtures?
"So? I've always been a friendly, outgoing person."

9. Do you spend a lot of time reading romance novels?
"They make me feel good."

10. Do you sometimes compare your husband unfavorably with other men?
"He doesn't know, and I'll never tell him."

If your answer is Yes to any one of these questions, you are sending out signals unbecoming to a chaste, godly woman. Your sexual interest should be centered on your husband only. If it is not, you can be sure that other men will pick up your appeal like bees to a blossom. You are headed for trouble.

ACT LIKE A LADY

"But among you there must not be even a hint of sexual immorality, or of any kind of impurity, or of greed, because these are improper for God's holy people." (Ephesians 5:3) The only place for sexy clothes and seductive behavior is in your own marriage with your own husband. Act like a lady with every other man you encounter so that he will treat you like a lady. If he does not honor you in this way, give him a look that says, "Drop dead, Buddy," then walk away, head held high.

I have watched many a husband wince at his wife's flirtatious behavior and my heart sorrowed silently for him. She has embarrassed him. If he brings it to her attention in the privacy of their home, he will no doubt receive a full account of his own shortcomings. So he pretends not to notice, or pretends to think she is cute, in order to keep the peace. Wives, let us heed the wisdom of Proverbs 12:4, "A wife of noble character is her husband's crown, but a disgraceful wife is like decay in his bones."

TWO POWERFUL FORCES

Sex and money. Money and sex. These two powerful forces fit hand-in-glove. They are the subjects of most best-selling novels today, most movies, most television mini-series, and indeed most lives. Our hedonistic world plunges headlong after the pleasures to be had from sex and money.

God's Word hits this prevailing attitude squarely head-on. Note that in the above-mentioned verse, Ephesians 5:3, "sexual immorality" is linked with greed. That is, sex and money. In Colossians 3:5,6 we read, "Put to death, therefore, whatever belongs to your earthly nature: sexual immorality, impurity, lust, evil desires and greed, which is idolatry. Because of these, the wrath of God is coming." Because of the ungodly lust for sex and money.

God's way is purity and contentment. "Marriage should be honored by all, and the marriage bed kept pure, for God will judge the adulterer and all the sexually immoral. Keep your lives free from the love of money and be content with what you have because God has said,

Never will I leave you; never will I forsake you." (Hebrews 13:4,5)

There it is, specific instruction in the Word regarding sex and money. Yet I have seen many couples falter and fail because of their struggle in this area.

THE BEDROOM/BANKBOOK CONNECTION

Scene One: Charlotte feels her emotional needs have never been met by her husband Ron, who totally spends himself on his career. Since she does not get his physical stroking, she strokes herself with what his money will buy: the gorgeous designer dress, the Ethan Allen sofa, lavish lunches at "Chez Francais," and tennis lessons at the country club where she is a privileged member.

Bills mount, along with frustration on Ron's part, because he works himself to a frazzle, yet never comes out ahead at the end of the month. Tension escalates in the marriage due to the bedroom/bankbook connection. Ron feels unappreciated, unloved. He wonders why Charlotte can't be content. Why were they so much happier when they were young and just struggling to get by? Where is the reward of a loving wife for all the hard work he has done?

Scene Two: Phyllis and Ben were so head-over-heels in love that they decided to marry in spite of the protests of both their families. The parents had counseled waiting until Ben finished law school at least. But Phyllis assured everyone that she did not mind working to put Ben through school. Of course since she was bringing home the paycheck, Phyllis also wielded the power of the purse in this fledgling marriage.

After two years of financial dependence on his wife, Ben finally received his degree, passed the bar exam, and headed for the high-powered legal profession. They rejoiced over attaining their goal. As they celebrated over a candle-lit dinner, Ben pledged that Phyllis would never have to sacrifice again.

Soon they realized that there was more sacrifice required. Junior partners were expected to keep hours more befitting slaves until they proved their worth to the firm. But that was Ben's problem. Phyllis felt she deserved a good rest. She began to slouch around the house all day, slowly letting her face and figure go to ruin since she no longer worked out in public. In college days, Ben had shouldered much of the housework load, but now he never had time or energy even to carry out the garbage. Phyllis experienced a major role shift and was not too sure she liked it.

Meanwhile, Ben was surrounded every day by fascinating work and fashion-conscious women. As his salary grew, so did his image of self-importance. He began to feel the need for a more glamorous wife. Looking at Phyllis, he saw a frumpy housewife with two whiny kids. She constantly complained about his lack of attention, never realizing it was symptomatic of a deeper problem.

One tragic day Ben told her, "We have grown apart over the last few years. I'm sorry to tell you this, but I want a divorce. I've fallen in love with a woman at the firm who understands me in a way you never have."

"After all I've done for you?" Phyllis screamed.

How many times have you heard *that* story?

Scene Three: Brenda is a pouter. When she pouts, she makes life miserable for everybody, especially George. If there ever was a long-suffering husband, it is George. Sometimes he is still amazed that pretty, popular Brenda chose to spend her life with good old George.

What Brenda really chose to spend was good old George's money. As the son of a wealthy farmer, George always had plenty of cash to spend on her. This was supremely important to Brenda, whose father rarely had two nickels to rub together. So George brought the power of money to the marriage, and Brenda brought the power of sex. She often bragged that she could get anything she wanted out of her husband. If she pouted long enough, she could be sure of that trip to Bermuda or the gold bracelet or the red sportscar she wanted. Brenda had perfected her pouting. It was more than downcast eyes and quivering lower lip. She brought the added dimension of denying George his bed privileges until frustration finally made him knuckle under to her wishes.

God never intended that this basic urge He put within us be used as marital blackmail. In fact, He expressly forbids it. "The husband should fulfill his marital duty to his wife, and likewise the wife to her husband." We are not talking kitchen duty here. Let's continue. "The wife's body does not belong to her alone but also to her husband. In the same way, the husband's body does not belong to him alone but also to his wife. Do not deprive each other except by mutual consent and for a time, so that you may devote yourselves to prayer. Then come together again so that Satan will not tempt you because of your lack of self-control." (I Corinthians 7:3,4) The wife who shuts off sexual tenderness toward her husband is being disobedient to the Word of God. She is also playing with fire. She may find her husband's passion burning for someone else before long.

WHEN TO ABSTAIN

There are acceptable times of abstinence, of course. Times of illness. The last stages of pregnancy. Tours of military duty. Business travels. And spiritual withdrawal for fasting and prayer. During such times as these, we must remain absolutely faithful to our partners, even though the enemy will set up temptations. Remember, "The Lord knoweth how to deliver the godly out of temptations." (II Peter 2:9 KJV)

In my personal opinion, there is one other important time that a woman may withdraw from the marriage bed: when she knows her husband is having an adulterous affair. If her husband does this, he breaks his marriage vows and severs the binding ties. All through the Word you can see how God hates adultery. In His Ten Commandments for living, He strategically placed "Thou shalt not commit adultery" as Number Seven, right between the evils of murder and theft. (See Exodus 20.) It is astounding to realize how many husbands who would never steal and certainly never kill *can and do* commit adultery.

I am speaking here of the "double-dipping" husband. He wants both his wife *and* his mistress. He does not want to lose his family, his respect among his peers, or his upstanding reputation. Yet he is too beguiled by the other woman to end the affair. I have seen wives in this predicament, and it is dreadful. Desperately afraid of losing their man, they begin to compete with the mistress for their own husband's affections. In so doing, they lose all self-respect. Their dignity is stripped away as they grovel for the answer to what will please that man.

Before God, he cannot have both of you! Make him choose. If he does not choose for wife and covenant and honor, he is not worth having in your bed. Hard words, yes, but I am heartsick over the escalation of adulterous behavior which is shredding the very fabric of family life. The New Testament Christian is to be a one mate Christian. The pattern of Christ and the Church is our example for marriage. Paul said in II Corinthians 11:2, "I am jealous for you with a godly jealousy. I promised you to one husband, to Christ, so that I might present you as a pure virgin to him."

We *must* find answers to this increasing problem of infidelity, instead of merely shaking our heads and saying "tsk-tsk."

Obviously such a decision must be covered with much prayer and counsel. You need to be vitally connected to a body of believers where you will receive help and support through such a time as this. Also, I highly recommend Dr. James Dobson's book *Love Must Be Tough* which directly addresses this problem.

MY PSALM OF LOVE

If your heart has been broken, turn to Jesus. He came to heal your broken heart. He loves you.

If you feel dirty or used or abused, call on Jesus. He gave His life to make yours new. His blood washes away every stain on your soul. He loves you.

If you cannot show love to others because of a damaged past, reach out to Jesus. He will deliver you from those bonds that keep you tied up in knots. He loves you so much!

If your life is wonderful, the sun is shining, your lovingcup filled to the brim, then give thanks with a grateful heart to God. He is the Giver of all good gifts.

This is our supreme reason to live a virtuous, chaste, pure life: to please God our Father. After all He has done for us, how can we give Him anything less?

My Psalm of Love

Dear Father God,
Throughout my life You've been my Guide,
Eternal blessings You provide:
My loving husband, precious son,
You gave for me Your Only One
To bring me life and love and peace,
To heal my heartbreak, give release
From chains of sin to wings of light.

You set my feet on paths so right
And banished terrors of the night.
You're always there still loving me
Faithfully, so faithfully.
Even if I turn away
Your love comes reaching every day.
Thank You, Lord, for this great love.
Your rainbow banner waves above
My daily life for all to see—
With awe and praise I ask, "Why me?"
Comes rolling back from Heaven's throne
His joyous words, "My child, My own."

CHAPTER
7

MAKING A HOME

"to be keepers at home"
Titus 2:5

In the course of our travels over the past thirty years, Robert and I have been invited into hundreds of homes. It generally takes us about two minutes inside the front door to ascertain whether or not we have come into a real home. Not every house is a home. We have seen houses masquerading as homes when in reality they were Showcases or Museums, Warehouses or Workshops, Grand Central Stations or Hotels Bedlam, and even a few that could have been mistaken for Garbage Dumps!

THE SHOWCASE

Noreen proudly took me on a grand tour of her newly-decorated house. As we peered from the doorway into the pale green living room with its perfectly matched sofas, silk hangings, and carefully placed objects d'art, I felt I was seeing an illustration for "House Beautiful." It was beautiful! But that is *all* it was, a beautiful room for her to show. Nobody ever used that room. No one ever snuggled down into the soft sofas to enjoy a cozy chat. No one ever pulled aside the silk drapes to see a robin through the window. And I dare anyone ever to pick up one of those elegant crystal pieces to catch the sunlight and splash rainbows across the room.

The whole downstairs was the same. Gleaming silver sat on the sideboard of a beautiful dining room where no one ever ate. Floor to ceiling shelves were stacked with all the "right books" in a spacious library where no one ever read. Lovely white wicker furniture and expensive, exotic plants (changed monthly by her local florist) filled a sunny garden room where no one ever sat. Only in the kitchen and family room did we sense the reality of everyday life. The rest was simply a blueribbon showcase for Noreen's decorating abilities.

THE MUSEUM

I knew that Lynn and Cary were quite wealthy, so I wondered what a house would look like when price was no object. I anticipated lush beauty with every creature comfort. Instead, I entered a contemporary art museum featuring a vast expanse of white stone walls and floors. Further on, a greenhouse effect was achieved by glass walls overlooking a manicured atrium. Hard, uncomfortable modern sofas and chairs in subdued colors were flanked by marble tables and shuttered windows. Collections abounded. A collection of Wedgwood, that costly white-on-blue china; a collection of paintings, mostly oil, mostly jarring; a collection of boxes made from semiprecious stones; a collection of Boehm birds, those beautiful porcelain creations; a collection of safari treasures, including a real zebra skin rug; a collection of rare books, leatherbound, handtooled, gilt-edged. The whole house fairly shouted, "Don't touch!" Need I ask if any small children were ever invited to that house? I was to discover that Lynn herself was much more comfortable with lovely things than with lovely people. Her house certainly reflected that stark, distant feeling.

Making A Home

THE WAREHOUSE

Have you ever known someone who simply cannot throw anything away? Meet Janice. She is memorabilia's cousin. Janice is totally convinced that she must not discard that old hulahoop or the rusty box-springs from her first bed or the broken cuckoo clock which never did keep correct time. If she does throw it out, she fears she will suddenly discover a need for it. Janice has inverse reasoning at work here: so long as she keeps things, she will never need them.

Therefore, Janice's house is stuffed with stuff and junked with junk. She still has maternity dresses and baby clothes though her youngest child is nine years old. "You never know when a little surprise may come along." She has boxes of scrap fabric dating back to her high school days. "Someday I'll make a quilt with all kinds of memories on it." She has every Christmas gift, birthday present, and anniversary memento she ever received whether she liked them or not. Each drawer, closet, shelf, and niche in her house is cram-packed. Her double garage is stacked to the ceiling with countless boxes of everything under the sun. With one great garage sale she could finance her daughter's entire college tuition, plus books and parking fees. The pervasive feeling in this type of house is clutter, not comfort.

THE WORKSHOP

Chris is a creative, talented lady. She loves to sketch and is learning to weave. She makes lovely musical instruments called dulcimers. She quilts. She has just taken classes in china painting. She can do candlewicking and cross-stitch and needlepoint with equal ease from her own original patterns. Chris likes to do all these things simultaneously.

A visit to her house was most interesting. I always took care not to wear suede, lest I leave covered with bits of yarn, fabric, or string. Chris greeted me at the door, removed her paint-spattered smock, and led me into the house. We could not sit in her living room because she had shoved all the furniture to one side to set up her easel at the bay window. The wobbly-looking card table standing nearby had an assortment of charcoals, pastels, oil paints, turpentine, and china plates. Canvases in various stages of completion were propped against the walls. "It's the only place in the house with enough decent light for me to paint by," Chris explained the clutter airily as she led me on to the den.

This room had her loom sitting right in the middle of the floor, with a work in progress on it. Baskets of brightly colored yarn sat around the loom waiting their turn at the shuttle. I admired her weaving while she hastily brushed wood shavings off the chair which she scooted over to me. "I was carving on a dulcimer last night, and I forgot all about this mess," she said. Chris had not invited me for lunch, which was just as well since her dining table was totally obscured by the quilting frame which hung above it. There was a beautiful "Rose of Sharon" quilt on it about half completed.

I wondered where in this house her husband and children carried on their business of living. In their bedrooms? All the visible part of the house was totally covered with Chris's creative projects.

THE GRAND CENTRAL STATION

This is a fascinating type of place to me, although I certainly would not like to live there. A Grand Central Station house is just what the name implies, a central place where people rush around making connections on their way to other places more important. It is filled with a constant whirl of busy activity. You get the feeling no one really lives there. They just buzz in to get their messages, change their clothes, and grab a bite to eat before dashing off to their next appointment. They are generally a bit breathless from all the rushing, yet they always seem to run at least five minutes behind schedule. Quite often the members of this type family will go for long periods of time without spending a meager ten minutes together as a whole family unit. One rushes out the door as the other hurries in. They tend to leave a lot of notes taped to the refrigerator.

Many families live this way nowadays. Take the Malones, for example. Mr. Malone is in sales, so he travels every other week. He offices at home when he is in town. His business phone rings a lot.

Mrs. Malone teaches at an elementary school all day and runs a cosmetics business out of her house in the evenings. She has her own telephone which also rings a lot. They have two teenagers, seventeen-year-old Susan and fifteen-year-old Craig, who both go at life full-tilt.

Susan is a captain on her school's drill team, senior class Student Council representative, Teen Fashion Board member of a prominent department store, and second year dancer in the city's Junior Ballet Troupe. She fits in part-time modeling jobs where she can, and she plans to enter several beauty pageants as soon as she turns 18. "All that scholarship money, you know."

Her brother is a blossoming photojournalist. He is very involved with the school newspaper and the yearbook. He goes to every sports event, camera in hand, and spends hours on end in the school's darkroom. Craig works part-time at Burger King, mostly to finance his hobby. "Do you know how expensive lenses are?" And he enters every photography contest he can find. A good-looking, personable young man, Mark is popular with girls and guys both. Any time he has at home, besides sleeping, is usually spent on the telephone.

The Malones devote no time at all to family togetherness. All their interests and energies are directed "out there" to the places they feel are important enough to be always scurrying off to.

If you asked, "Do you all love one another?" they would be astonished, perhaps even indignant. Yet they never take time to show their love. No time to worry over Dad's loss of the big client so long as he can still pay their charge accounts. No time to realize Mom is bone-weary as she faces yet another huge load of laundry and sixty papers to grade. No time to discuss those emotional pressures building up inside each family member. No time to have quality communication with the Lord or anyone else. No time, no time, except for the unending demands of things "out there."

THE HOTEL BEDLAM

This is the kind of place I can endure for about fifteen minutes before I must make some kind of escape. It is a madhouse! In the Hotel Bedlam there is every kind of noise imaginable. The television has never been turned off, ever. It chatters continuously, whether anyone is watching or not. One child has his stereo blaring away at 600 decibels, while the other tries to drown the sound with her radio. The smaller child and her friends run through the house slamming doors, shrieking at the top of their piercing, little voices. Father bellows at everybody in general to "Knock it off!" Baby is crying for attention while Mother attends to the clattering washing machine. In Hotel Bedlam the appliances never run quietly. Dishwashers groan, hairdryers wail, blenders whine, air conditioners wheeze, telephones shrill. There is absolutely no peace to be found anywhere in the Hotel Bedlam. Even if you lock yourself in the bathroom away from the noise, soon someone will beat on the door with, "Can you hurry? I need to get in there."

Besides the potential threat of a 40% hearing loss, there is an even worse danger in living at Hotel Bedlam. The occupants may never hear the voice of God calling to them, directing their way. Rarely does God thunder at us. He chooses rather to speak in a still, small voice.

The Holy Spirit is like a gentle dove. We must learn to be quiet before the Lord if we expect to hear His voice. Jesus said, "My sheep hear my voice." (John 10:27 KJV) When we hear His voice, we follow His leading. But first we must *hear* it. The Lord instructs us, "Be still, and know that I am God." (Psalm 46:10 KJV)

Again in Isaiah 30:15,16, "In repentance and rest is your salvation, in quietness and trust is your strength, but you would have none of it. You said, 'No. . .'"

176

A house like Hotel Bedlam gives sure indication that the Lord's presence is not given priority there. In Isaiah 32:17,18 He describes the kind of home He provides: "The fruit of righteousness will be peace; the effect of righteousness will be quietness and confidence forever. My people will live in peaceful dwelling places, in secure homes, in undisturbed places of rest."

The Hotel Bedlam doesn't even come close.

THE GARBAGE DUMP

It is difficult to believe that seemingly normal, educated adults could turn their place of abode into a garbage heap. Yet this happens more often than you might think. During our college days Robert and I invited the couple next door over to get acquainted. We lived in a one-room efficiency apartment which had been built by unskilled carpenters during the WPA days. (The Works Progress Administration was a make-work government agency created as a Depression Days relief program.) But we had painted the little place, hung some dime-store curtains, put a couple of throw rugs on the floor, bought a few pots of ivy, used some of our nice wedding gifts as accent pieces, kept the place sparkling clean, and made the best of what we had. When our neighbors came to visit, they were visibly impressed with our efforts. Joyce sank down into our one good armchair and sighed, "Oh, this place feels good. It seems like home." I wondered what their apartment looked like. We soon found out. They invited us for dinner the following week.

My nose gave the first warning as Larry opened the door to greet us. The stench inside wafted out onto the evening breeze. My eyes gazed in stunned bewilderment at the sight spread before us. At least two weeks' worth of garbage was piled into open grocery sacks which lined the kitchen wall. Dog poop was scattered on papers all around the living area. Robert and I had to step gingerly. When we went to wash our hands, our pinched nostrils betrayed the fact that the bathroom had never been cleaned. Whew!

We simply could not believe the filth of that place. Heretofore, I had thought only ignorant slumdwellers lived this way. But Larry and Joyce disproved that theory. They were both candidates for their Master's degrees.

As she cleared off a space at her table, Joyce called us to eat. I glanced in panic at Robert who managed a wan smile of encouragement. I gulped hard, grabbed at my rising nausea and pushed it firmly back down, gathering my self-control. Silently beseeching the Lord to help me through this meal with grace, I also reminded Him that His Word promises, "If you take up any deadly thing it shall not harm you." (See Mark 16:18.)

Since that eye-opening evening, I have found that a great many people choose to live in Garbage Dump houses. Some former neighbors, for instance. He was an aviation engineer. She was a sociologist. They had five children, two of whom were near my son's age. The first time Kip went into their house, he experienced culture shock. It was his first visit to a Garbage Dump house. He tried to describe it. "Mom, you can't believe all the junk, piles of paper, boxes of stuff everywhere! There's no room to move—they just have little trails leading through the rooms. Their garbage can is sitting *open* in the kitchen, with bugs crawling around! There are greasy engine parts scattered around all over the carpet. I'm telling you, Mom—you'd just DIE!"

One time Kip summed up Garbage Dump houses very succinctly as we drove by that particular place. "I'll bet if they ever move out of there, scientists could go in and find twenty new kinds of mold, mildew, and fungus!"

Women who keep such houses as these would do well to heed Proverbs 31:27, "She watches over the affairs of her household and does not eat the bread of idleness."

All these different kinds of houses I have described are actual places where people live. But they are not homes. Not one of them, from the greatest to the meanest, offers the basic ingredients of a se-

cure resting place we long for in our homes.
What makes a house a home?

FROM HOUSE TO HOME

A real home opens its doors to you and says, "Be warm. Be welcome. Be blessed."
A real home has nothing to do with size or decor. It has everything to do with peace and comfort, security and acceptance, stability and permanence.
A real home extends the feeling of being glad you have come, being hopeful you will leave refreshed.
A real home is a place where you can come for help, knowing you will not be turned away.
Victor Hugo put it this way in "House and Home":

> A house is built of logs and stone
> Of tiles and posts and piers;
> A home is built of loving deeds
> That stand a thousand years.

MINI OR MANSION

We have been in real homes of many different types and spaces. In Jane's tiny one-bedroom apartment, we sat around the coffee table and ate her delicious *chicken a la king*. Though the space was limited, she welcomed us and loved us and blessed us with her hospitality. We shared good music along with good fellowship in her little home. It was not cramped; it was cozy.
We have also been in real homes which resemble palaces. At Anne's home a valet parked our car and a uniformed butler met us at the door. Our hostess genuinely welcomed us and presented us to

many influential people. That magnificent home was opened weekly for Bible studies and times of ministry. Those who came felt equally at ease snuggling into the soft sofas or curling up on the cushy carpet. They were blessed in sharing Anne's love.

Whether mini or mansion, yours can be a real home. It all depends on you, the keeper of that home. If you grew up in a real home and your mother was a good role model, it will be easy for you to establish this kind of place for your own family. However, many of you were not blessed with this kind of stability in your formative years. In growing up you may have been shifted from pillar to post with no real place to call home. Only a tentative feeling of "Well, I wonder how long we'll be here?" Now you may be longing deep within to build a stable home for your own family without having the faintest idea of how to bring it to pass.

Many young women today have suffered (through no fault of their own) their parents' traumatic divorce and the uprooting of their home, followed by the adjustment of living in a new place with a single parent. Then comes the shock of a remarriage to a stepparent who often brings new siblings into another new place to live. Stress mounts as parents and stepparents try to create a "blended" family unit.

Sometimes this pattern is repeated over again, leaving lives jumbled any which way, much like an impossible jigsaw puzzle. Who can put the puzzle together in a meaningful way so that all the cracks do not show, so that none of the pieces are missing, so that a clear and beautiful picture of life emerges? Only God Himself can do this. And indeed He has done it again and again through the miracle of His grace. He will work this miracle in your life if you open your heart and home to Him.

YOUR PLACE IS HIS PLACE

"Your Place" by John Oxenham puts it quite clearly:
Is your place a small place?

Tend it with care!–
He set you there.
Is your place a large place?
Guard it with care!–
He set you there.
Whate'er your place, it is
Not yours alone, but His
Who set you there.

Realize that your place *is* His place. Thank Him for the home He has provided and dedicate it to the Lord, literally and physically. How do you do this? Simply walk through every room in your house, turning it over to Him as you go.

"Lord, this is Your living room. Please help me make it comfortable and use it for Your glory.

"And Lord, here is Your kitchen. I really need Your grace here. Help me to enjoy preparing nutritious meals for my family. Let the cleaning-up never overwhelm me.

"In this bedroom, please help me to be the loving, exciting wife you planned me to be for my husband.

"Oh, Lord, help me rejoice to keep this bathroom sparkling clean."

You get the idea. If your husband agrees, you might even ask your pastor to come over one evening and pray a blessing, a covering of love on your home.

ANGELS AT EVERY CORNER

When Robert and I moved into a country home we had built, we invited several of our friends over for the house blessing. We asked a zealous young man, Jerry, who was a blazing star for Jesus, to pray the dedication prayer. I sat on the stairway and watched him pray. I shall never, never forget that prayer. Jerry blessed everything—I do mean *everything*—in our home. Even the support beams! He anointed the doorway with oil and blessed everyone who would ever pass through it. He posted angels at every corner. He covered it with protection from fire, storms, sickness, plagues, disease, and death. Talk about an insurance policy!

You may be smiling, but do you know it worked? That house has been blessed and protected supernaturally. When ministry called us back into the city, we had to leave our home to the care of its ministering angels. Each time we come back to it to rest or to write, we feel their presence and are blessed anew by their thoughtful protection.

Once you have dedicated your home to God, you may find cleaning it to be less of a chore. After all, you would not want to give God a dirty house, would you? My grandmother used to say, and then my mother said, and now I say, "People may not can help being poor, but there's no excuse for dirt. Soap and water don't cost all that much."

If you have several small children, or if there are other demands on your time, you might consider having someone come in to help you clean the house every so often. I have found a wonderful source of help at a local Bible School.

You may also find that once you have dedicated your home to the Lord, you suddenly have His help in furnishing it. Countless times the Lord has led me to find precisely the item I had needed, and usually it was on sale!

PINK AND GRAY

Several years ago Robert and I purchased a house in Dallas which was a complete "re-do." Although the place was a fantastic buy, it required long hours of sanding, painting, cleaning, stripping, varnishing, and so on to fulfill its potential. I had put off working on the bathroom until last, mainly because I could not decide what to do with it. I fervently wished I could rip it out and start over, but our budget did not extend to that. This bathroom was covered with ceramic tile in pink and gray. I realize that Art Deco has brought this color combination back in style recently, but at that time it was totally passe.

So I decided to emphasize the pink, hoping the gray would simply disappear. Pink towels and pink bathmats complemented pink soap in a pink soapdish, with pink tissue paper and a pink and white flower arrangement. I hung a white shower curtain inside the white tub which I planned to cover with a lovely sheer pink drape to hang outside the tub. That would complete the bathroom decor. No one would even *see* the gray.

One afternoon Robert informed me that he had invited a very special couple home for lunch the next day, Charles and Carolyn Simpson. It was time to find that pink drape. By noon tomorrow! I flitted off to the nearest shopping mall. However, there were no pink sheer drapes to be found. My heart sank as I went from one drapery department to the next. Finally I was ready to admit defeat when I did what I should have done first—I prayed. Simply, "Lord, You know what I need. Please help me to find it. Amen."

THE MIRACLE CURTAIN

Immediately I had the distinct impression that I should go over to the Custom-made Drapery department. I had thus far only looked in the ready-made areas. But the idea made no sense to me, as there was not time and certainly not enough money to have a drape custom-tailored for my bathroom by noon of the following day. Still that inner Voice kept urging me. Obediently I walked over to the department. There I saw a whole rack of custom-made drapes which had been unclaimed or rejected by the people who ordered them. Now they were on clearance at ridiculously low prices for such quality fabric and craftsmanship. Imagine my joy to see the pair of sheer pink pinchpleated drapes hanging there just waiting for me! A glance at the tag showed them to be the *exact* length and width and price to fit both my bath and my budget. Joyfully, I transported them home.

As we hung them in place I told Robert, "What God says about the hairs of our head all being numbered (in Matthew 10:30) has suddenly become very real to me. He obviously cares about even the smallest detail of our lives, right down to my bathroom curtain!"

When we sold that house, I left all the drapes in place, except one. The miracle curtain went with us. Today it hangs in another pink bathroom as a reminder of my Father's loving provision of "exceeding abundantly above all that we ask or think." (Ephesians 3:20 KJV)

Again and again God has shown His faithfulness as Jehovah-Jireh, the Lord God our Provider. I think He must not like junk, because He always helps us find quality items to meet our needs.

Perhaps you are looking around your room right now thinking, "I wish I could change this place but . . ." The buts usually fall into three categories:

1.   I don't know how.
2.   I don't have enough money.
3.   I'm afraid I'll make a mistake, so I'd better just leave well enough alone.

Let's address these reluctances one by one. First, "I don't know how."

THE NESTING INSTINCT

God has placed within each woman the nesting instinct. That desire in your heart to feather your nest is as natural as breathing. You can see it even in little girls at play. Four-year-old Stephanie picks wildflowers to grace her teatable for the party with her dolls. Six-year-old Susanna wants to plaster all your walls with her fingerpaintings and crayon sketches. Eight-year-old Ashleigh spends hours rearranging the furniture in her dollhouse, only to do it all over again the next month. These little darlings at play are really expressing God-given feminine characteristics.

Realize that you already have within you the capacity to create a beautiful home. No hired decorator can bring to your home the unique feeling of your own personality. You simply need to ask God's guidance and provision.

A WEALTH OF IDEAS

All around you, in every magazine you pick up, is a wealth of decorating ideas. As a place to begin, start a picture file. Each time you come across a picture of a room that really appeals to you, clip it out and slip it into your file. After several weeks of this, open your file and spend some time studying it. You will notice some trends.

Perhaps your choices tend toward a cozy, country look. If so, think what you can do right now with what you already have to begin moving toward country decor. Could you cover that bare wall with the quilt your grandmother made for you? Is it just tucked away in the closet right now? Could you hang some ruffled curtains at the window? Remember, you do not have to do everything at once. Just make a definite beginning, do something to show that you have charted a new course for the future.

Another good source of decorating ideas is help from friends. If you have a friend who is particularly gifted in creativity, ask her to walk through your house and give you some ideas. Every woman loves to feel her opinion is valued. You do not have to make every change she suggests, of course, but she might come up with an idea or two that you can really latch onto. Perhaps your friend has wished she could offer a couple of suggestions but has held back for fear of giving offense. I would love to have asked one dear lady to trash her black wrought-iron birdcage filled with orange plastic nasturtiums, but she never sought my counsel. If you want help, learn to ask.

Also, you must learn to see, really see. Observe your surroundings. Open your eyes. When I enter a home that reaches out to welcome and warm me, I pause to ask why. What is it about this place that I like so much? The color scheme? The comfortable chairs? The yummy smell of baking cookies, which turns out to be a vanilla candle? The soft background music? What? Obviously, the people in that home are most important, but the furnishings should reflect their love of life.

BUDGET DECORATING

Now let's look at Category Two, "I don't have enough money." You may never have enough money to do everything you'd like to do at one time. So don't wait until then. Go ahead and begin. Sometimes merely rearranging the furniture can give your home a fresh new look. Switch your lamps from room to room. Cover an endtable with pretty fabric. Check out a book from your local library on budget decorating.

How about trading some piece of furniture with a friend? That extra chest out in your garage might be just what she needs for her child's room. Would she be willing to trade something of equal value for it—perhaps a chair or rug or rocker?

One time we were given a massive Spanish dining room table and chairs. At the time we really needed a large table, so I was grateful for it even though I am not especially fond of Spanish furniture. Eventually we were able to buy a dining room set more to our taste. I traded the Spanish set to my bachelor brother who liked its dark, masculine look. In return, he gave me two traditional loveseats which were perfect for my needs.

Another time some friends of ours were moving into an apartment too small for their kingsize bed. So we traded them our smaller antique bed and dresser for their big bed with all its linens. You see, there are creative ways of changing your home. You do not have to rush out and spend, spend, spend.

Some people love shopping garage sales. "You never know

what you'll find," they say, "for one man's junk is another man's treasure." A word of caution here: Be sure what you buy is *not* junk. It is far better to spend your money on one new piece of quality furniture than to dribble it away on garage sale bargains. Once I showed a $2.00 lamp I had bought to a brutally honest friend who declared, "Yes, you get what you pay for." That is true. She was right.

THE PRINCIPLE OF SOWING AND REAPING

I am a great believer in sowing. You will find this principle throughout the Word of God. It is spelled out clearly in Galatians 6:7. Whatever you sow, you will reap that very thing. This principle applies to every area of our lives. If you sow honor, you will be honored. Sow caring and you will find others caring about you. Sow criticism, you will soon find critical fingers pointed at you. Whatever you want to reap in your life, that is what you must sow.

This is obviously a spiritual principle, but every spiritual principle has a literal, physical outworking as well. When we are planning to replace items in our home, we look for a place to sow into the lives of others. Remember, I am speaking of good things, *not* junk. No one is blessed by having junk dumped on them in the name of the Lord.

Robert once gave away the only two chairs I had in our living room. A young couple who had just moved to Dallas for a fresh start had no chairs at all. They were thrilled with those rust-colored armchairs. However, all we had left to sit on was the sofa. Immediately the Lord provided funds for two new occasional chairs, a beautiful wingback chair, and an easy chair with ottoman. They were all on sale, I might add.

Another time we gave our dining room furniture to a large family who had lost almost everything through financial reverses. All we had left to eat on was a little dropleaf table with barely enough room for our three place settings. A few days later, that great Spanish dining set I mentioned earlier was sitting in our dining room. It is truly amazing to see God's hand at work in the sowing/reaping principle. We do not give in order to get. "Giving to get" is not true sowing. We simply sow into the lives of others to bless them, and it is fascinating to watch the crop grow. The Lord always gives back *more* than we gave away.

As I said, this principle works in every area of our lives, even clothing. Once a family came to our church in desperate straits: no job, six children, ragged clothes, broken-down van, no place to live, all hope gone. Believe me, this was a worst case scenario. We immediately began to minister to them in every way. I asked Marie, an older woman who came to church occasionally, if she had a couple of nice dresses she could give to the mother of this family since they were about the same size. Her reply stunned me. "Why should I give my clothes away? They are too good. When I get tired of them, I can put them in a garage sale and make some money." And that was that! My heart grieved for Marie because in all her Christian walk she had never learned the high cost of selfishness. She had planted no seeds. I knew the day would come when she needed help and kindness, but there would be no crop for her to reap. Now in the sunset years of her life, Marie is an unhappy, unhealthy, pinchpenny woman. She who sows sparingly shall also reap sparingly. (II Corinthians 9:6)

But she who sows bountifully shall reap bountifully. What a wonderful promise this is! We all have things we can share with the needy. Think of those clothes you haven't worn in over a year, way back there in your closet. Yes, they are good things, but you are not using them. Why not bless someone who *would* use them?

FARMER IN THE KINGDOM

Every so often I do radical surgery on our family's wardrobe. Those clothes we are not wearing (except for sentimental items) I send to the Loaves and Fishes Ministry to be distributed among believers in need. We ought to minister first to those of the household of faith.

(Galatians 6:10) Then we must help the poor and strangers with the gleanings of our field. (Leviticus 19:9,10)

The first time I did this, I will never forget what happened. I sent two large boxes of clothing over to Loaves and Fishes a few days before we went to a conference. At that meeting a man I hardly knew took my husband aside and asked permission to give me a gift from the Lord. Robert consented, of course. Who would turn down a gift from the Lord? Obviously it was a gift of money, since he handed me a small, brown envelope. But what he said was to the point, "The Lord wants you to spend this on some lovely new clothes, whatever your heart desires." Inside the envelope were two crisp one-hundred dollar bills.

This sowing/reaping effect has been proven true so many times in our lives that I am becoming a regular "farmer" in the Kingdom. I love to see those crops come in. I challenge you to try it. Instead of moping about not having enough money to upgrade your home, sow a few good seeds in fertile ground and wait for a fascinating return.

CREATIVITY UNBOTTLED

The Third Category of excuse I mentioned was, "I'm afraid I'll make a mistake, so I'd better just leave well enough alone." What a sad choice. You would let fear keep your creativity bottled up? Let insecurity rob your family of blessing? Let doubt triumph over faith? Remember Philippians 4:13, "I can do all things through Christ which strengtheneth me." (KJV) Please memorize this promise and call upon it as often as need be.

Work up a plan of how you want your house to look. Then work out that plan little by little as you have time and funds. Do not set your plan in concrete. Adjust it as you go along to fit the changing needs of your family. This year's darling nursery should look very different by the time your child starts to school. What served as the

TV/guestroom in our house at one time is now a lovely formal dining room.

It is very important to use every area of your house. Do you have one room that is just a catch-all. Why? That is valuable space you are paying for every month. Throw away the junk, sow the good items and clothes, open up that room. What does your family really need in that area? A playroom? A TV room so you can remove your television set from the conversation area? A sewing room? A study for homework? A workshop for Dad? Put that space to good use.

STEWARDS OF THE MASTER'S BLESSING

Using every part of your home in this way means being a good steward of the things God has given you. He is pleased with our good stewardship of His blessings. When we read Jesus' story of stewardship in Luke 19, we see that those who used the master's blessing wisely were given approval and reward upon his return. However, the servant who did nothing to improve or use that which was left in his charge greatly displeased the master. He was reprimanded severely, and his privileges were handed over to the servant who had made the best use of what he had.

God expects us to *use* what we have. To use it in service for Him. That is why He gave it to us in the first place. Every good thing you own, right down to the very body you live in, has been entrusted to you by God the Father. (James 1:17) When we are good stewards, He rewards us with more and more blessings.

There are abundant ways you can use your home for the Master. Let me list a few:
• Start a neighborhood Bible club for the children around you.
• Invite a different person or family in your church over for fellowship each week.
• Have a ladies' prayer meeting. Or exercise class.
• Keep a young mother's small children one afternoon a week to give

her some much needed quiet time.
• Bring home two or three elderly ladies who live in a nursing home for an afternoon excursion outside their confining walls.

This list could go on infinitely, but those are some practical ideas of using your home for the Lord. He told us, "Inasmuch as ye have done it unto one of the least of these my brethren, ye have done it unto me." (Matthew 25:40 KJV) Think of every person you bless in your home as blessing our Lord Himself. Isn't that tremendous? All those little things you do for others that no one notices and that seem insignificant, you may be sure Jesus takes note. You have done them for Him.

OPEN HEART, OPEN HOME

From the time we had our first little apartment, Robert and I have used our home for the Lord. That one-bedroom place was a refuge for the inner-city teens Robert taught. They came to glimpse a different world from the filth and crime of their own ghettos. We gave them love, food, counsel, and hope for a better tomorrow.

From there we moved into a rented house which gave us an extra bedroom. That room housed a wide spectrum of guests. Gloria was a soft-spoken kindergarten teacher who needed a home until she could afford her own place. At the other end of the scope came a foulmouthed hippie who had totally lost his way. Our home is available to anyone the Lord brings to us, even "the least of these."

HOMES FOR BLESSING

As we used our home for Him, the Lord kept moving us up into better places. Next we were able to buy our own house, and from there we went to a home on a lake which we loved. It is worth mentioning that we always shared that lakehouse. We were traveling in ministry at the time. So on the weeks we were scheduled to be gone, we opened our home to others. Newlyweds honeymooned there. Tired ministers and missionaries came to rest and be refreshed. Young families on tight budgets had wonderful free vacations. And in due time the Lord blessed us with land, ten acres of woods where we built the country home I mentioned earlier.

Not all of the experiences were positive, I hasten to add. After all, people are people. Sometimes they were thoughtless. Certainly the ghetto children were. They had no manners at all. Sometimes our guests were intrusive, poking into things which were not their business or plopping down in the middle of our private conversations. Sometimes they were forgetful to leave money for their long-distance calls. Some did not replace the Charmin. Accidents happened, so a few things were broken. But for the most part, the blessings and benefits far outweighed the minor events. The Lord kept on blessing us.

All of this was always done with an extremely limited budget. I cannot tell you where the money came from to feed all these people and house them, except that God provided every extra dime we needed, many times in totally unexpected ways from completely different sources. It was almost like having a secret bank account, drawn upon the Bank of Heaven.

ROSEMARY'S REWARD

I *know* people wondered how we managed. Some of them were bold enough to ask. Like Rosemary.

Rosemary was a bold, brassy beautician. She had only visited our church a couple of times when she came to our home. What a disaster that could have been! The moment she walked through our front door, her heavily mascaraed eyes began darting to every object in sight, appraising its worth. I could almost hear the cash register ring up the total in her brain. I invited her to sit down. As she plopped into the nearest chair, she breezily commented, "Boy, I'll be glad when I get rich so I can have a house like this."

Is she being nasty, I wondered, or merely trying to be funny in a crude way? Doesn't she realize that our small church can pay only a meager salary? Defensiveness welled inside me. I wanted to retort, "Why should God give you a better home? You're not using the one you have now for anything but your own selfish purposes." But I bit my tongue and opted for kindness instead. Realizing that here too was God's precious jewel, although a bit roughcut, I began to gently polish. I recalled for her how the beautiful staircase wood had been given to us by a friend who was closing his hardware business. As I shared stories of how we had acquired some of the lovely antique pieces, I kept emphasizing the principle of sowing/reaping and good stewardship of God's gifts. Hope began to dawn in her purple-smeared eyes as she grasped the idea of seeking first God's kingdom.

A few Sundays later, she offered her home for a time of fellowship after the evening service. Then she asked if a regular prayer meeting could be held there. She's learning, I smiled inwardly. She knows to do good and she is doing it. What was her reward?

The desire of Rosemary's heart had been to have her own beauty shop. As she put God's plans into effect in her life, she was soon given her heart's desire, Mountain Valley Hair Fashions. God's principles are eternal, everlasting. They *do* work!

Never be afraid to open your home. And please do not wait until it is all "just right" before you begin blessing others. Keep it clean. Make it as lovely as you can. And share it with others. In doing so, you share it with Jesus Himself.

Beautiful words of James Russell Lowell that I learned in high school poetry class come back to me often:

Not what we give, but what we share,
For the gift without the giver is bare.
He who gives of himself feeds three:
Himself, his hungering neighbor, and Me.

CHAPTER 8

FOR GOODNESS' SAKE

The stately buildings still sparkled in their Christmas finery, twinkling gold and green, white and red. We were showing our friend Jerry Stanley beautiful downtown Dallas as we took him back to his hotel. Jerry had once been intensely involved in our lives as director of my television program, but that time seemed long ago and far away. He was in Dallas to direct a major New Year's Eve musical event which was televised nationally.

Over fine Mexican food, we caught up on the events of the intervening five years which had passed. Laughing over guacamole dip, we recalled fond memories. We shared fajitas and faith. We talked of the goodness of the Lord. To the sound of mariachi music we pondered the future still before us.

ISLANDS OF STABILITY

Just before we parted, I tossed a question to him. "Jerry, in the five years since you've seen us, how have we changed?"

He shook his head and smiled. "You two never change," he replied. "You're like islands of stability in seas of confusion." I felt it was the greatest compliment I had ever received.

My prayer has always been that I would be found faithful. "Now it is required that those who have been given a trust must prove faithful." (I Corinthians 4:2) We who have been entrusted with the marvelous gift of God's grace *must* be faithful.

ON THE SOLID ROCK

All around us people are stumbling and falling. Some who walked in God's light for years have turned back to grope in darkness. There are those whose sins have been flaunted by the media in such a tragic way as to bring shame and disgrace upon the Church of the Living God. Leaders have betrayed their followers. Marriages that seemed so secure have shattered. Nowhere does there seem to be solid ground on which to stand.

Oh, but there is!

The lyrics from a favorite old hymn *The Solid Rock* by Edward Mote declare it:

My hope is built on nothing less
　　Than Jesus' blood and righteousness.
I dare not trust the sweetest frame,
　　But wholly lean on Jesus' Name.
　　　　On Christ the Solid Rock I stand.
　　　　All other ground is sinking sand.
　　　　All other ground is sinking sand.

In this shaky world of ours, people are groping for stability, for dependability, for reality. Goodness, pure and simple, is being able to show them Jesus in our lives. Giving them a Rock on Whom to stand. We cannot *be* that Rock for our loved ones, only Jesus can. But we can be faithful. We can be dependable. We can be trustworthy and true. We can be there when they need a friend. We can pray. This is goodness.

In order to show the goodness of Jesus Christ through our lives and lifestyles, we must behave in ways that are stable and predictably good. The most mature, steady believers I know are those who respond with goodness in every situation. I may not know exactly *how* these friends will face a crisis, but I can predict that it will always be good. I know they will hear both sides of a matter. They will not be rocked off balance. They will not succumb to gossip nor rumor. They will think the best of everyone concerned. This is goodness.

A framed piece of art I purchased recently has two lovely ducks crossing a pond, with these words, "Behave like a duck. Stay calm on the surface, but paddle like crazy underneath."

OUTWARD SIGNS OF INNER GOODNESS

Serenity. Faith. Trust. These are the outward signs of inner goodness. Inwardly we may be fighting a battle of faith, but we do not mope around or wallow in self-pity. To all outward appearances, we are steady as she goes. "My heart is fixed, O God." (Psalm 57:7 KJV) "He shall not be afraid of evil tidings: his heart is fixed, trusting in the Lord." (Psalm 112.7 KJV) Calm. Poised. Chin up, heart hopeful. Truly beautiful. The women in my family had a specific criterion for beauty: "Pretty is as pretty does." Have you ever heard that one? It was the standard response to any question about looks.

"Granny, don't you think Mary Ethel is pretty in her new dress?"

With a smile, "Pretty is as pretty does."

"Mother, I'm bound to be pretty when my braces finally come off, don't you think?"

Wisely, "Pretty is as pretty does, honey."

Their guiding principle of life was always goodness. Good manners, good morals, good friends were more to be desired than popularity or position. Goodness was never to be sacrificed on the altar of peer pressure. No matter how beautiful a woman was, she ruined her appearance to others if she did not behave like a lady. Real beauty was always measured by a woman's goodness.

In fact, we are instructed over and over in God's Word to do good. "Therefore, as we have opportunity let us do good to all people, especially to those who belong to the family of believers." (Galatians 6:10) "Trust in the Lord and do good; dwell in the land and enjoy safe pasture." (Psalm 37:3) "Therefore to him that knoweth to do good and doeth it not, to him it is sin." (James 4:17 KJV)

BARRIERS TO FORGIVENESS

Goodness is a fruit of the Holy Spirit. (See Galatians 5:22.) It has very practical outworkings in our lives. One of the main qualities inherent in goodness is the capacity to offer forgiveness. This is desperately needed in our world today. Goodness seeks to make peace and urges others to do the same. Goodness does not burden itself by carrying grudges. Families have literally been destroyed over petty problems which should have been forgiven and forgotten long ago. But wounded pride, coupled with the need to be right, threw up barriers to forgiveness. What a tragedy! We are told, "Live in peace with each other. . .encourage the timid, help the weak, be patient with everyone. Make sure that nobody pays back wrong for wrong, but always try to be kind to each other and to everyone else." (I Thessalonians 5:13-15) This is goodness.

GREG'S STORY

Gregory, one of Kip's friends, sat at our kitchen table watching me cook dinner. He was a moody young man, but that was understandable since this sixteen year old lived with a lot of tension at home. I kept a gentle patter of conversation going while he decided whether or not to open up. Finally the dam burst.

"I *hate* my father!" Greg angrily declared. Since he called his mother and stepfather by their given names, I realized he must be referring to his natural father who had walked out on this young son many years ago. What on earth had happened to break open those old wounds? Gregory angrily continued, "Last week I went to see my Grandma who lives in the same town as my real dad. I decided I wanted to see him–just to see him. So I drove over to his house. I knocked on the door and some strange lady answered. When I asked about my dad, she said, 'Oh, he moved out about two years ago. I don't know where he went.' I felt like such a fool. Two years! He didn't even let me know he was gone. That woman must have thought I was some kind of idiot, coming to see a dad who'd been gone two years, and I didn't even know it."

My heart ached for Greg. Rejection by a father is a deadly blow to any child. The fathers who have abandoned this present generation of children will have much to answer for when they stand before God to give account of their deeds. (Revelation 20:12)

"Greg, all I can say is you have to let go of it. Please forgive your dad and let God wash away the pain you feel. Remember, when you grow up and become a dad, remember how you feel now so that you'll never, never walk out of your own little boy's life."

Watching our young friend struggle through adolescence, sometimes with periods of violent behavior, we loved and counseled and prayed with him as often as we could. Late one night he showed up at our door with a gun. Thrusting it into my hand, he pleaded, "Keep this for me right now. I'm afraid I'm about to do something stupid." He knew our home was a safe haven for him. Again we talked to him about the cleansing blood of Jesus and the power of forgiveness, but he would not let go of the bitterness of his past.

One morning a desperate-sounding Greg called, "Can I come over? I've gotta have help."

His grandmother had died. He was on his way to her funeral where he knew he would see his dad for the first time in years. "I've called him every name in the book. I've planned to cuss him out in front of everybody. I've thought of everything I can do to humiliate him at his own mother's graveside. And the more I plan, the worse I feel."

We sat in our living room and talked about forgiveness: what it does, how it frees, why it must be given. Robert read Jesus' story in Matthew 18:23-35 about the man who had been forgiven such a huge debt, yet he would not forgive another man just a paltry amount. That one who would not forgive was turned over to the tormentors for punishment. It is still true. Those who will not forgive create a prison cell for themselves in which they are tormented day and night.

Finally Greg released his long held bitterness against his father. With many tears his soul was washed. When he met his dad at the funeral he was able to conduct himself in a civil, courteous manner. He overheard his father tell his mother, "Our son turned out to be a fine young man, didn't he?" One positive word, only one, from this man who should have been there for Greg through the years. But considering the scenario Greg had envisioned earlier, this was quite a victory.

Goodness lets go. It realizes that holding onto past hurts is like chaining yourself with weights which sap all your strength.

In every sad family struggle, there must be a peacemaker. Remember, Jesus said the peacemakers get the blessing. They will be called the children of God. (Matthew 5:9) Someone has to be the first to reach across the breach, hand extended in reconciliation. Why not let that someone be you?

This is goodness.

Goodness makes time and room for the hurting Gregs of this world in moments of crisis. Your home may be the only safe place they know. Please don't turn them away.

> 'Tis the human touch in this world that counts,
> The touch of your hand and mine,
> Which means far more to the fainting heart
> Than shelter and bread and wine;
> For shelter is gone when the night is o'er
> And bread lasts only a day,
> But the touch of the hand and the sound of the voice,
> Sing on in the soul alway.

> —Spencer Michael Free, 1856

It has been ever thus.

A TOUCH OF GOODNESS

Caring for others, reaching out is what goodness means. Goodness never centers on self. It looks at the world around with caring eyes. It lightens the load of weariness. It touches the downcast and lifts up their heads in renewed hope.

If there was ever a need for touching, it is today. Our world is so fragmented. People live under heavy stress. The touch of a friend's hand means so much. Don't you love it when a friend notices you're sagging a bit so she massages your tired shoulders? Doesn't it lift your spirits when a child says, "I need a hug"? We respond to human touch. Studies have proven that babies left isolated with no human touch will shrivel and eventually die, even if they receive food and sustenance. Touch is that important!

Jesus constantly reached out to touch people. Matthew 9:27-29 recounts how He healed two blind men. He could have called down laser beams from heaven to restore their sight. But He chose to touch them with His gentle, healing hand.

"When he came down from the mountainside, large crowds followed him. A man with leprosy came and knelt before him and said, 'Lord, if you are willing, you can make me clean.' Jesus reached out his hand and touched the man. 'I am willing,' he said. 'Be clean!' Immediately he was cured of his leprosy." (Matthew 8.:1-3) Do you realize the significance of Jesus' touch on this leprous man? Lepers were outcasts, untouchables. There is no telling how long it had been since the poor fellow had felt the touch of a human hand. No doubt the large crowds following Jesus drew their breath in awe as they saw His courage in putting His hands on a leper. Surely they gasped in amazement as the man's skin changed from deathly leprous white to natural healthy flesh. To be touched by Jesus this way in front of crowds of people must have made up somewhat for those bitter months of having to cry, "Unclean!" when he entered their midst.

It does not take great skill or training or wealth to be used by the Lord in this area of goodness. We simply must have a listening ear to go where He bids us and do what He says. He knows when and where our touch is needed.

SPECIAL DELIVERY FROM THE LORD

The day before Easter, 1990, I was in a dark, deep valley. So
many things had gone wrong in my life that I began to feel God had
withdrawn His presence from me. My mother had just come through a
long illness. No sooner was she well and on her feet again than my dad
was diagnosed with cancer. The building plans we had for Prayer
Mountain in Dallas were on hold due to lack of funds. It seemed I
heard discouraging words on every hand. I was lying down in our
bedroom in a kind of twilight of the soul when Robert burst through
the door. "Jo, come here! Look what Mary Ann has brought."

Mary Ann Brown is a delightful, godly woman who ministers
all over the nation. We rarely see her, but when we do she always has
an uplifting word. She was carrying a *huge* bouquet of gorgeous flowers: gladiola, snapdragons, lilies, carnations, and fern. It was the big-
gest basket of flowers I have ever seen. She said, "We just had our
youngest daughter's wedding. As I was carrying out these flowers, I
felt the Lord telling me to bring them to you. I wasn't even sure which
house was yours, but the Lord said He'd show me. Sure enough, as I
drove down your street, I saw Robert out in the yard. So, here are your
Easter flowers, Special Delivery from the Lord."

Hope welled up in my heart as I thanked her for her obedience
and told her how much it meant. The Lord had not forgotten me!
Knowing how much I enjoy flowers, He had sent me an abundant reminder of His love for me.

Outwardly, nothing had changed. But inside my heart, renewed
confidence grew that God would get me through this valley too. When
my faith was faltering, He sent Mary Ann to show me He was still
right there beside me.

FROM SHADOW TO SUNSHINE

We made it through that dark time. Life has its days of shadow,
but if we just hang on and don't lose hope, we come out into the sunshine sooner or later. My father lived eight more full, happy years.

My mother is healthy, happily tending her garden, busy at her needle-work. The beautiful house of worship on Prayer Mountain has been completed. We press on through. "And let us not be weary in well doing: for in due season we shall reap, if we faint not." (Galatians 6:9 KJV)

How grateful I am that Mary Ann took the time to show goodness to us. It made all the difference.

It helped me hold on and "faint not."

GOODNESS IN ACTION BACKSTAGE

Another time I saw goodness manifested in a caring way was when my son reached out. It happened at a Margaret Becker concert. For several years Kipling was the keyboardist for Margaret, a contemporary Christian artist. After their concert in Dallas, I had gone backstage to see my son. Just at that moment, Tom Autry walked up. Tom is a gifted songwriter and singer who often ministered at our country church when Kipling was just a lad. Though his music was wonderful, somehow Tom had never gained a very wide audience. Now there he was, wistfully standing on the edges, looking at the little kid who played with his synthesizers now grown up and playing to thousands of people. "Hey, Kip," he called, "remember me?"

Success did not spoil my son. His goodness reached right out and enveloped the lean musician, his long-ago friend. "Tom! Tom Autry! Man, it's great to see you. Do I remember you?! You're the main man who got me started on this music track. I'm so glad you're here! Hey, Margaret—Margaret—come here, you gotta meet this guy . . ." I was so pleased my heart nearly sang. My son's gesture meant so much. It was goodness in action.

You may be asking, how do you know when to do something or where to go? Goodness simply takes the opportunities extended to it. Mary Ann had a huge basket of flowers she wanted to bless someone with, so she asked the Lord, Who? And He told her. Kip had opportunity to lift the spirits of a tired musician by recounting the blessing he had been and presenting him to a popular artist. These were small acts of kindness in themselves, but they were of great significance in the lives of the recipients.

Sometimes we get so immersed in the busyness of daily life that we fail to see the needs around us. Or perhaps our own problems have grown so tall that we cannot see over them. Jesus cautioned against this in His parable about the sower of seed in Matthew 13. "The one who received the seed that fell among the thorns is the man who hears the word, but the worries of this life and the deceitfulness of wealth choke it, making it unfruitful." We must not allow the cares of life or the concern over money to divert us from being involved in the Master's business, to go about doing good as He did.

SUDDENLY UPSIDE DOWN

One of the hardest times of my life was when our son broke his leg in the church nursery. He was only eighteen months old at the time. Because his little bones were growing so quickly, he could not wear a cast. The orthopedic specialist deemed that both of his legs must be put up in traction so that they could continue to grow at the same rate while the fractured leg was healing. So they strung up my screaming baby, feet in the air, legs wrapped tightly with bandages, shoulders just barely touching the bed. Pitiful sight! Even passing strangers would stop to look. Kip was traumatized, his world suddenly upside down. I was distraught. I continuously called on God to speed up the healing process, for the doctor told me we would be there at least six weeks. The very thought of it was overwhelming.

After two weeks I put my faith to the test. I asked Dr. McAmis to X-ray Kip's leg, just to see if he might be healed already. The doctor firmly shook his head. "We can do the X-ray if you like, but I can tell you what it will show. The bone will be in place to heal, but there has not been enough time for calcium deposits to have formed yet. We can't take him out of traction until that happens." I stubbornly clung to the shreds of faith I had left and insisted on the X-ray. *Please God, please, please let my baby be healed.*

The technician made the X-ray. The results were exactly what the doctor had predicted. My hopes plummeted into despair. Robert had to leave for a ministry trip. Mother had to return home after two weeks of helping me. I was left alone to cope with this.

A CHANNEL OF HIS GOODNESS

After crooning Kip to sleep that night, I crumpled before the Lord. Finally I stopped demanding my own way. I prayed what Catherine Marshall called "The Prayer of Relinquishment" in her book *Beyond Our Selves*. This is where you just let go of what you really want, throw yourself on the Lord's mercy, and say, "Not my will, but Thine."

"Alright, Lord, I have done everything I know to do. I have prayed, believed, called others to join their faith with mine, insisted on the X-ray in the face of my doctor's obvious disapproval. I've tried everything I know to try and nothing has worked. Here we are still facing four more weeks of this miserable hospital life. I give up, Lord. If You want us to endure another month here, then I simply ask for Your grace to get us through. Go with us, Lord, because I cannot make it on my own. My strength is gone." And I sat there before Him, totally spent.

Sounds of sobbing wafted into the room, floating in from across the hall. Compassion welled in me, for I had shed many tears myself in those past few days. I quietly rose, followed the sounds of grief, and entered the room where a woman lay weeping. Walking to her bedside, I softly asked, "Why are you crying? Can I help?"

Quickly she turned to me in the dim light. "Oh, I am so afraid," she cried. "I'm having surgery in the morning and I'm just so scared!"

"Would you like me to pray for you?" I asked.

"Oh yes, please," she gasped, like a drowning woman grasping a lifeline.

I laid my hand gently on her shoulder and began to pray. As I asked the Lord to send the Comforter to her, I felt her begin to calm. I spoke Psalm 23 softly, "Yea, though I walk through the valley of the shadow of death, I will fear no evil: for thou art with me; thy rod and thy staff they comfort me . . . Surely goodness and mercy shall follow me all the days of my life . . ." By the time I said "Amen" she was totally at peace.

She looked up at me wonderingly and whispered, "Are you an angel?"

I smiled. "No, I'm the lady across the hall whose little boy is strung up in traction. Now get some rest. The Lord is with you."

During that brief encounter when I reached out to help someone else, something wondrous happened in my baby's room. Just three days later enough calcium deposits had formed in Kip's leg that he was released from the hospital! Three days instead of four weeks! God gave us our miracle when I focused outward to someone in need, when I became a channel for His goodness.

I share that very private time only to encourage you to keep reaching out. Look for the opportunity God presents to you. Be involved in the world around you. Join the PTA, work on the Fall Festival, coach the Little Soccer girls, join the neighborhood co-op. Don't allow your life to become narrow and boring. The more you are a part of the lives of others, the more opportunity you will find for showing the love of Jesus to them.

FROM THE OLDER TO THE YOUNGER

A real need in the Body of Christ today is for spiritual mentors: that is, older women who will offer counsel, guidance, and encouragement to younger ones. Role models. The days are gone when women were surrounded by mothers, aunts, and cousins. That support network has crumbled, due to a highly mobile society and women in the work force.

The Church must begin to fulfill this need. Every person in the Body of Christ has a place of ministry. The older women are instructed to teach the younger ones. That is the thesis of this whole book. But many older women say, "I've raised my kids. I don't want to raise anybody else's." Thereby they lose the opportunity to extend goodness and reap a great reward.

When Mother was a part of our ministry before she and Daddy moved to South Texas, she had a vital impartation into the lives of many young women. She taught them to sew, to make pies, to bake fresh bread for their families. She reproved them when they were selfish, encouraged them with the Word when they were blue, and prayed them through their trials. She made Easter dresses for their little ones and enchiladas for their husbands. They loved her for it. Mother was a spiritual mentor to them.

Today I see many young women whose own mothers have no input into their lives (due to distance or death). Those of us on down the road of life need to impart wisdom to them. We must begin to care. Take time to encourage when the breast-feeding is painful. Take time to keep the children when she is frazzled and needs a few hours of quietness. Take time to reassure when the teenager is trying her patience. Take time to comfort when her husband loses his job and the debts are mounting up.

In order to reach out and be a blessing, we must try to lead a positive life. I have a little sign above my desk, "When Momma ain't happy, ain't *nobody* happy." How true. If we are negative and discouraged, we communicate that to everyone around us.

POSITIVE IN A NEGATIVE WORLD

How do we stay positive in an increasingly negative world? By seeing ourselves through a Kingdom focus. We are daughters of the King, placed here in this world to do His will. To maintain a consistent positive attitude we must have a daily prayer life and praise time in His presence. When we spend time with the Shepherd of our souls, we find goodness and mercy following us all the days of our lives. As we move in this anointing, we have the grace to care for those who need our loving touch.

If you have not developed the habit of a consistent, daily time with the Lord, please begin now. I promise you it will make a remarkable difference in your life. You will begin to find His Word coming alive in you. When a friend calls to complain, you'll have a Scripture verse that will speak directly to her need.

There are many fine daily devotional guidebooks. Pick up a copy of "Streams in the Desert" or "My Utmost for His Highest." This will give you a place to begin.

Fill your home with praise music. Recently a great number of beautiful praise and worship albums have been released. Good music lifts the spirit.

I emphasize that good books and good music are only tools to help your devotional life. The vital link is connecting on a daily basis with the Lord who loves you, who gave His life for you, who desires for you to live in victory. Take the time to talk to Him. Then listen to Him. Remember, He speaks in a "still, small voice." You can please Him by obeying His voice, whatever He tells you to do. You may think it is just a small thing. "To obey is better than sacrifice." (I Samuel 15:22 KJV) No doubt He will ask you to reach out to others with a touch of goodness. Your touch matters. Your life counts in the Kingdom of God.

One of the sweetest songs of recent years was written and sung by Ray Boltz. It is simply called "Thank You." In this ballad he dreams that he is standing in Heaven with his friend when various people begin to give thanks for the goodness shown to them.

Thank you for giving to the Lord,
I am a life that was changed.
Thank you for giving to the Lord,
I am so glad you gave.
One by one they came
Far as the eye could see,
Each life somehow touched
By your generosity.
Little things that you had done,
Sacrifices made,
Unnoticed on the earth
In Heaven now proclaimed.

Here in life, goodness is its own reward. But some day the

books of Heaven will be opened. "Behold, I am coming soon!" declares our Lord Jesus in Revelation 22:1 "My reward is with me, and I will give to everyone according to what he has done."

I trust that when He opens the book to your name and mine, He will find countless deeds of eternal goodness.

CHAPTER 9

THE GREAT DIVIDE

"to be obedient to their own husbands"
Titus 2:5

On a dark, lonely road in the middle of the night, I learned the importance of submission. After an extremely busy time of ministry in the city, I was going to the Hill Country to rest. Robert would follow a couple of days later. I had eagerly looked forward to this time away. Earlier as I had packed, I kept having to field telephone calls and other busy intrusions. The daylight began to fade. Finally Robert had said, "Honey, I think you ought to wait and leave in the morning. I just don't feel at peace about your heading out into the darkness."

Stubborn me. "Robert, I'll be fine. I'll drive straight down there and not even stop. The car is serviced and ready to go. I'm all packed. And you know if I wait, my tomorrow will get filled up just like today. I want to go down *now*." So I overrode his counsel. At that time I did not think of it as the Lord's word to me. I was about to learn a severe lesson.

I drove through dusk and fading twilight, into gathering darkness. Around 10:30 p.m. I turned onto Hoffman Lane, a winding country road which led to our house about fifteen miles away. Suddenly the engine of my little red Charger just died. I eased the car over to the shoulder and coasted to a stop. I tried the ignition again and again. Nothing. The car was absolutely stone dead. There was no response whatsoever. Not even a click.

A FLASHLIGHT AND A STRONG TOWER

I was stranded, miles from any house, from any phone, from any source of help on a dark country road. The hushed night noises from the surrounding woods pressed in on me. *Dear God, what am I going to do?* I grabbed a flashlight, locked my two puzzled puppies in the car, and started walking. "Lord, if I ever needed Your help, I need it now. Please, please send someone to help me. I know it's the middle of the night, and I know I shouldn't even be out here on this lonely country road by myself. I repent for not listening to my husband. Oh God, I'm so *scared*!"

No sooner had I uttered these words than a pair of headlights appeared far down the road. "God, please let these be good people. I cast myself on Your mercy, Lord." The Word I clutched was "The name of the Lord is a strong tower; the righteous run to it and are safe." (Proverbs 18:10)

An old, battered pickup pulled alongside me. Crammed into its front seat were four *braseros*, Mexican nationals who cross the Texas border to find work. They were all holding cans of Coors. I grasped my meager Spanish and tried to explain my predicament. They all got out, poked around under the car's hood, shook their heads, and then offered me a ride to the nearest phone.

What a choice! Get into a truck with four beer-drinking men or keep on walking. I chose to walk. I thanked them kindly for stopping, then turned to walk away. The leader called out to me, "Por qué no va con nosotros?" ("Why won't you go with us?") I didn't want to tell them the real reason, that I was scared out of my wits. So I gestured that there was no room for me. The four of them were all riding up front. Gallantly, three of them swung out of the cab into the bed of the truck. Still I shook my head and kept walking. "Señora, Señora, por qué?" Finally I decided to get honest with them.

Tremulously, I replied, "Por qué tengo miedo." ("Because I am afraid.")

They were genuinely astonished. Quickly they offered reassurance in the darkness, "No, no, no! Somos amigos." ("We are friends.")

It sounds ridiculous now, but I just could not spurn their kind offer of help. Clutching my faith, "Lord Jesus, this better be the help You've sent me or I'm in big trouble," I climbed into their truck. Believe me, I do not recommend that any of you ever do this, but it seemed right at the time.

THE NEAREST FARMHOUSE

The driver pointed down the road. "Una casa, alla," indicating that we would go to the nearest farmhouse. It was about two miles back down Hoffman Lane. Do you know how much praying one scared lady can do in two miles? We turned into the driveway, by a mailbox which read "Faust." Grimly I smiled, recalling Goethe's story of the man named Faust who sold his soul to the devil. It seemed to fit right into this nightmare.

Mr. Faust came to the door in his striped pajamas. He peered out at me suspiciously while I told my tale of woe and begged to use his phone. Finally, reluctantly he admitted me into his farmhouse where I called a friend to come rescue me. Then I waved a thankful "Adios" to my four Mexican knights in their old truck.

When I finally collapsed on my bed that night, I admonished myself tearfully, "JoAn, don't dwell on what could have happened. Just be grateful for the grace of the Lord."

Of course when my husband heard of my wild adventure, he

nearly went through the roof. My dad about had a heart attack. My son pointed out how fortunate it was that I could speak some Spanish.

Robert drove down the next morning, had the Charger towed to a garage where we learned the alternator had gone out. So that was the reason Robert had "a check in his spirit" about my heading out into the night, although we did not know it then. We call it a check in the spirit when we feel some hesitation or warning, even though there is no rational reason. I can tell you that after my frightening ride through the night, I listen far more keenly to my husband's counsel.

THE HEAD OF YOUR HOUSE

That's what submission is: choosing to honor your husband as the head of your house by submitting to his authority. It is an attitude of the heart. "Wives, submit to your husbands as to the Lord. For the husband is the head of the wife as Christ is the head of the church, his body, of which he is the Savior. Now as the church submits to Christ, so also wives should submit to their husbands in everything." (Ephesians 5:22-24) When we choose to submit to our husband's leading, we are doing it as to the Lord. That is the way He chose to establish order in the family. Somebody has to be the final authority, and God decided it should be the husband. He is the one who will have to give account to the Lord for how he handles the lives given into his care. God stated His reason for choosing Abraham to be the father of His people, "For I know him, that he will command his children and his household after him, and they shall keep the way of the Lord, to do justice and judgment." (Genesis 18:19 KJV)

Yet many times we wives balk.

In fact, some godly women who are perfectly at peace with every other Scripture in the Word of God simply dig in their heels at those which speak submission. They quote in rebuttal, "There is neither Jew nor Greek, slave nor free, male nor female, for you are all one in Christ Jesus." (Galatians 3:28) And "God is no respecter of per-

218

sons." (Acts 10:34 KJV) This is certainly true. In the Kingdom of God, women are not second-class citizens. We all stand equally before God regarding our salvation and Christian walk, our giftings and graces.

GOD'S PATTERN FOR FAMILIES

Our God is a God of order. When He hung the worlds in space, He established perfect order. He set the ecological system in balance. He made the tiniest atoms to function precisely.

And His order is also established in the family of mankind which He created. "Your desire will be for your husband, and he will rule over you," God declared to Eve after her colossal, eternal mistake. (Genesis 3:16 KJV) The submission God requires of wives is simply that of yielding one's rights to a higher authority. No inferiority is implied at all. "Now I want you to realize that the head of every man is Christ, and the head of the woman is man, and the head of Christ is God." (I Corinthians 11:3) As Christ is in authority over man and is therefore to be honored by man, so the husband is in a position of authority and is to be honored by his wife. This is the pattern for Christian families.

Everything functions more smoothly when there is a definite leader in charge. Yet so many times there are real power plays in marriage. If a wife's "truster" has been broken in her childhood by an alcoholic or untrustworthy or shiftless dad, she may need true inner healing before she can submit to her husband. If she watched her parents divorce in a bitter battle and felt utterly abandoned when Daddy walked out, she will have difficulty believing that her husband really has her best interests at heart. If she was violated by incest as a child, as one in four little girls are nowadays, she must be dealt with gently and tenderly all her life.

Then there are those of us who are strong-willed with an "I know best" mentality. We must have our minds renewed by the Spirit in order to be able to walk in this realm of submission.

You see, God established submission for our *protection*, not as some kind of heavenly put-down. God cherishes women. He wants us to be cared for and nurtured. He made us to be the carriers of life, the highest honor ever bestowed on humanity. Only God Himself can give life, but He put within woman the place of nurturing and bearing new life. He gave to us the honor of continuity of generations. Without us, all human life would come to an end in one generation.

To our husbands He gave the responsibility of governing. So for every Scripture about our submission, there is an equal charge to our husbands to love and nurture and cover us. The three verses I quoted earlier from Ephesians 5 are followed by *nine* verses directed at our husbands on how to love us and take good care of us. The key to all this is understanding the honor-bound covenant of marriage so a wife knows that her husband cherishes her above all others and wants only the very best for her.

Sometimes our husbands even have to love us enough to let us fall on our faces, as did Robert when I went driving off into the night. But the Lord uses those times too, to prove to us the validity of submission.

Let me emphasize that submission is an attitude of the heart. You may be outwardly meek and docile while inwardly seething and rebellious. In other words, you might be sitting down on the outside, but by Crackies you're still standing up on the inside!

This attitude will not work over the long haul. Truth will out. Always. And it usually comes out at the most volatile time, spewing repressed emotion over everybody in sight.

TALK ABOUT THE "TOUCHY" THINGS

If you think your husband is unreasonable in his requests, sit down and discuss it calmly. Let him know that you have his best interests at heart. Reaffirm that you are the helpmate God gave to him, so you want to be all that he needs in a wife. But if you have really tried to rise at 5:00 in the morning, to be dressed and coiffed and have waffles sitting in front of him by 6:00 and you just cannot do it all, then *tell* him. Don't sit around fussing and fuming about how unreasonable he is.

When you love one another, you work things out. You compromise on things that don't really matter, while you work harder on those things that do.

The problem with most marriage relationships is that the two people don't talk about the real issues, the "touchy" areas. If you would only talk it out, calmly, rationally, and hear his point of view, you might be surprised to find out things which have bothered him for months and affected his opinion of you are things you can easily change.

Just don't get defensive. And if he reacts in a negative, defensive way, tell him, "Hey, wait a minute—I'm on your side here. We're in this together. Let's work it out, because I want what is best for both of us."

Suppose he really *is* wrong? You have looked at the issue up and down and sideways, and every inner instinct tells you this is not going to work the way he has it laid out. What do you do then? Close your eyes and blindly plunge along beside him into failure?

Not at all. Remember, you are his *helper*. Don't argue or nag or whine or plead. In the most positive way you can think of, explain the pitfalls of his decision that you see ahead. When he shoots down every one of your objections, it's time for some heavy duty praying. You might even try fasting. Ask the Lord to send some godly men that he trusts to speak to him before it is too late.

Many times Robert has embraced truth spoken by his male friends when I had tried to tell him the same thing only the day before. Again, this has to do with the flow of authority.

I can rejoice that he finally heard the message, or I can pout because he didn't listen to me. Which is preferable? "I have resolved that my mouth will not sin." (Psalm 17:3) Not even "I told you so." Help us, Lord.

THROUGH THE REFINER'S FIRE, TOGETHER

If, after all your prayer and fasting, all the godly counsel your man has received, he resolutely sets his jaw and goes forward with his bad decision, then you go with him. God knows your husband must need this experience, because He could have averted it. So pray grace upon yourself and quick understanding for your mate. It will not be a happy time. In fact, I can almost guarantee it will be most *unhappy*. But hang in there, like the good helpmate God called you to be, and you both will get through it. Let God take you through the refining fire and purify your hearts.

I know whereof I speak. One time I was required to follow Robert into a situation where I was absolutely miserable. When I look back over our lifetime of marriage, I see this time as the lowest point in our years together. Yet it was a necessary time for us.

My precious husband had been deeply wounded in a church situation. In fact, he was so troubled he even doubted his ability to hear clearly from the Lord. Another minister came along and convinced Robert that they should start a church and be "Co-Pastors." All kinds of alarm bells went off inside me. But this man was urbane and highly educated and quite mellifluent. So he convinced Robert to give it a try.

What was I to do? Stay home and pout on Sunday mornings? No, I swallowed my pride and submitted to my husband's decision.

It soon became evident that we two couples did not fit together. In fact, we saw everything from two different points of view. Even our cultural heritages were worlds apart. They were rock-ribbed Yankees. We were born and bred Southerners. I soon became discouraged over how the services were conducted. All the women were strongly urged to wear a head covering. Not a hat, but a kind of lacy doily which just covered the tops of their heads. Many of the women wanted to dance during the very extended praise and worship time. Most of them took off their shoes and waved their arms in the air. We were required to stand for exhaustingly long periods of time. I am not saying that this was wrong. I am happy for people to worship in whatever way best fits them. It did not fit me, and I was made to feel less than holy by my failure to participate.

Robert never required any of this from me. It was the women who exerted pressure on me to conform. I was miserable. I looked for an honorable way out. I decided to begin a Children's Church in conjunction with the morning service. This was partly as an exit for me, and partly due to concern for my son. Just a child, he was bewildered by this new type of church we were attending.

Finally Robert realized that the idea of "Co-Pastors" which sounded so good in theory simply did not work for us. The other man's opinions always prevailed. Robert began to seek the Lord for deliverance from this very sticky situation. I cried a lot in private and put on a brave face in public.

STRETCHED TO THE BREAKING POINT

Finally I reached the point where I could take no more. I cried out, "Lord, save me!" God is so gracious to answer our heartcries. He sent two different men, two good friends, to visit us. Both René Brown and Cleddie Keith told Robert, "Friend, your little wife has stretched about all she can stretch. If you don't get her out of this situation very soon, she will probably snap." That was all it took. Suddenly Robert's eyes flew open and he began to really *see* how miserable I was. He resigned the next week, and we were out of there within a month.

As I said, sometimes we need these unhappy experiences. They build mettle into our character. Robert has since looked back on that time as a great turning point in his life. Never again would he allow another man to determine the course of his ministry. Never again would he get involved in a pursuit where his own wife could not stand gladly at his side. He also pauses now to Stop, Look, and Listen, when my alarm bells start clanging. He knows I really am his helpmate, because I walked through the fire with him.

THE UNBELIEVING HUSBAND

Obviously I have been discussing the behavior of godly husbands here. But what if your husband is not a believer? What if he requires ungodly things of you, such as wife-swapping or aborting an unplanned baby? What should you do? Meekly bow your head and follow him to hell? Peter addressed this problem in I Peter 3:1,2, "Wives, in the same way be submissive to your husbands so that, if any of them do not believe the word, they may be won over without words by the behavior of their wives, when they see the purity and reverence of your lives."

Your behavior should be that of purity and reverence. You are not expected, in my opinion, to flout the laws of God in order to please an ungodly man. I know there are teachers who differ with this stance. But I believe that our highest allegiance must be to our Savior and Redeemer. Remember, I am talking about being asked to do evil. Gently explain to your husband that to do evil would violate your inner being. Don't push God and the Bible at him, for this will only make him angry. But be firm in refusing to do evil.

So we have come to a place where submission does *not* extend. Submission does not mean slavery. You are not a doormat for your husband's muddy feet. Submission does not require you to remain in a dangerous situation where a drunken mate uses you as a punching bag or violates your teenage daughter. Submission does not require you to be stripped of all dignity and self-esteem as a woman. God loves you too much for that.

LAYING DOWN AUTHORITY

Since World War II, women have been culturally conditioned to be independent. The Equal Rights Movement and the feminist agenda have sold women on the idea that to be dependent on a man is archaic. "Today we are strong and self-sufficient. We stand solidly on our own two feet, making our own choices." I have heard many young women declare, "I'll never let any man tell me what to do."

Added to this cultural layer of independence is the fact that most women today are involved in the business world. Many of them are in management, telling others what to do all day, making decisions, giving opinions and input. How easy is it to lay aside this mantle of authority when you walk into your husband's presence? Difficult, at best. Those of you who move daily in positions of authority must take care to lay down your role of "boss" at home.

When I produced the children's television series "Backyard," I officed in our home so I would always be available to my family. But when I flew to California for the taping and stepped onto the set, I was the boss. I had the final say over the whole program. I always welcomed advice from my director, but if I did not like what he suggested, we changed it. I readily began to see how this could be a real trap. Power is heady, and it is highly corruptible unless it has divine reins. There was always a kind of clutch period when I returned home, readjusting to Robert's leadership and laying aside my power of final authority.

I have a friend whose husband salutes and calls her "Sarge" when she begins barking out orders. That pulls her up short. You see, her husband travels abroad for two weeks at a time. So she has to make all the household decisions in his absence. Life goes on. When he returns, he takes the leadership of the family back in hand, so she can relax.

SOW HONOR NOW, REAP HONOR LATER

You know the consequences for disobeying authority. You run the red light, you pay the fine. As the inner city kids say, "You do the crime, you do the time." This is true in the arena of family life too. If you dishonor your husband by constantly being at odds with him, challenging all his decisions, and generally sowing disrespect, then you will soon find yourself reaping this same crop from your children. Sassiness, backtalk, disrespect in abundance. Where did it come from? Check your attitude of submission to your own spiritual authority, your husband. If you sow honor, you will reap it.

Most of the time submission is easy. In fact, we rarely even think about it. Only when it challenges our own desires does it become a struggle. This is where Jesus' admonition "Whoever loses his life for my sake will find it" (Matthew 16:25) comes into reality. When you lay down the struggle to get your own way, you are thereby honoring the Lord as well as your husband. The Lord will reward you for your righteousness.

THE TEARS OF OBEDIENCE

One of the hardest acts of submission I ever struggled with was the time Robert felt called to leave our country home and move back to the city of Dallas. We had been pastoring an idyllic little country church with a charming name, the Church in the Wildwood, out in the Texas Hill Country. We had developed a camp there and a Bible training school. The home we had built was a dream-come-true nestled by a brook in ten woodland acres. I planned to stay there until Jesus came.

Wrong. In about four years Robert strongly felt his time of ministry in the Hill Country was at an end. The Lord wanted him to go to Dallas where the need for ministry was so much greater. "Oh, no, Honey, are you *sure*?" The more we prayed about it the surer he was.

I did not want to go. I shuddered to think of taking our twelve-year-old son away from his sheltered environment and plunging him into the perils of a big city school. I cried when I thought of selling the only home we had ever built. I walked in the woods and patted the trees and called out to the Lord for confirmation that this was *truly* what He required of us. That confirmation came, unmistakably. I asked for another sign, one that was almost impossible: to sell our office building for cash within two weeks. It happened. Obviously we were going to Dallas.

We never considered keeping our country home because we knew how expensive city life would be. In order to buy a home there, we figured we had to sell the one we owned. So we put our beloved home on the market, signed it away on a "Contingency" contract, packed up our household, and headed for Dallas. Our cat Shasta and I were both simply miserable.

THE REWARDS OF OBEDIENCE

Settling into life in the city, I tried not to think about the house I had left behind. But I was reminded every month by the mortgage payment. You see, the contingency contract fell through, so we had to keep the mortgage payments current. Every month we barely squeaked by financially. Four months passed, and still the house had not sold. Finally one night just as the clock struck 1:00, Robert heard me sigh, rolled over in bed and asked, "Are you still awake? What are you thinking about? The Hill Country house?"

"Yes," I replied. "How did you know?"

He snapped on the bedside lamp. "Because it's been on my mind too. We have a fair price on that place. It has been shown dozens of times, yet not sold. Do you suppose the Lord wants us to *keep* it?"

I sat bolt upright in bed. "Oh, Honey, could we? Do you think?" Then my practical nature asserted itself. "But how can we? The April payment is due right now."

We sat there thinking. Finally Robert decided, "We have two vehicles, my old classic truck and your Cougar. Let's put an ad on both of them in the paper on Friday. If one of them sells before the weekend is over, then we'll know the Lord is keeping our house for us. We'll have the money for the payment."

I lay back, delighted, thrilled to think, Could it be? Was the

Lord really not going to make me sacrifice my place in the woods now that I had been obedient?

The ad appeared in the Friday morning paper. There was not one call on it all day Friday. Nor Saturday. Nobody seemed to want a white Econoline pickup or a red Mercury Cougar. My hopes plummeted.

Sunday morning before I was even awake, the telephone rang. The caller told Robert he wanted to come over right then and buy the truck, it was exactly what he had been looking for. "But the bank is not open today," Robert countered. The man said he was a cash buyer and he had the money right there in his hand.

"JoJo," Robert patted me awake gently. I opened my eyes to find one hundred dollar bills fluttering down over the bed.

"What is this?" I gasped, startled awake.

He smiled. "It's your Hill Country house."

SUBMISSION: YOUR CHOICE

From that day on we never again had a struggle making the payment on the country house. God always faithfully provided, until it was completely paid for. We think of it as our retirement place. But it is more than that to me. It is more than a retreat, more than a place to write and rest. It is my reward for submission to God's will and my husband's leadership.

God does reward those who are obedient to honor His Word. Why not give it a try? Remember, submission is an attitude of the heart. It is a choice that only you can make. I assure you that if you choose *for* God's principle of honoring your husband it will make a major, wonderful difference in your life.

The poet Ella Wheeler Wilcox expressed the importance of our decisions this way:

> One ship drives east and another west
> While the self-same breezes blow.

228

The Great Divide

'Tis the set of the sail and not the gale
That bids them where to go.

Like the winds of the sea are the ways of fate
As we voyage along through life:
'Tis the set of a soul that decides its goal,
And not the calm or the strife.

CHAPTER
10

HOME IS WHERE THE HEART IS

"For where your treasure is, there will your heart be also"
Matthew 6:21

D eep in the heart of San Antonio, Texas stands a battle-scarred, beautiful mission. The Alamo. This rugged old fortress evokes a poignant feeling in the soul of every Texan who sees it. The Alamo was where one hundred fifty brave men chose to make their stand against tyranny in the face of incredible opposition. Over six thousand elite troops commanded by the Mexican Dictator Santa Anna surrounded the Alamo, calling for surrender. The gallant Texans chose to stand, to fight for freedom. They fought. And they died. Every single one of them. Including my great-great uncle, Jacob Darst.

Courage must have flowed through the veins of my forebear. He owned a small general store outside the town of Gonzales. In front of his store was a cannon which he had used for protection from intruders. When the Mexican government sent out an edict that the Texas settlers must surrender all their arms, Uncle Jacob went out and hung a sign on his cannon, "Come and take it!" After a failed attempt to come and take it, the Mexican army decided one small cannon wasn't worth

233

all that much trouble.

When Col. Travis realized how overwhelmed were his few forces against a huge Mexican army that stretched out on all sides, he sent out an urgent plea for help. Uncle Jacob Darst responded to that cry. He gathered a group of men, and under cover of darkness they entered the Alamo, going to a certain martyr's death.

After the Alamo fell, Sam Houston and his forces used the memory of those gallant soldiers who died as a rallying cry to other Texans. "Remember the Alamo!" That battle cry was a tonic to weary warriors. They fought and won freedom for Texas, thereby insuring that those men who gave their lives at the Alamo had not died in vain.

This slice of history is one of the treasures of our home. As a small boy, Kip was fascinated by it, wanting to hear the story again and again. "Mom, I wish they could have won," he would remark wistfully. He loved to go to the Alamo and see the painting of his ancestor. He felt a definite link with the courage of that long ago uncle. It is part of his family heritage, passed down through my mother, Eva Darst Holder.

YOUR FAMILY TREASURES

What are the treasures of your family? Have you ever thought about it? Have you given yourself and your family a sense of value in the grand march of eternity? A sense of worth and wellbeing that there is no other family in the entire world exactly like yours? Do they know about their family heritage? Have you made them aware of their unique place and time in history?

As Esther's uncle told her, "Who knoweth whether thou art come to the kingdom for such a time as this?" (Esther 4:14 KJV)

God has a unique plan for each person's life. All that we are today has been shaped by those who have gone before us. Good, bad, indifferent, our family forebears have had a vital influence upon the person we are now.

Give your child pride in his heritage. Everyone has someone special in his ancestry. Let him know he comes from good stock. Tell him that the courage or kindness, honesty or strength shown by that Great-granddad is in his genes today. In a world where families are fracturing at unparalleled rates, secure your children with love and family character.

Seek to maintain close contact with your child's grandparents, with your own parents. So many families today are completely estranged. This robs children of that sense of continuity, of seeing the familiar family traits.

I remember when Kip realized that his Grandmother Summers is a good artist. His Uncle David paints beautifully, as does his Aunt Helen. And his own father's paintings grace many of the walls in our home. Suddenly it dawned on him, "That's why I like to draw. Nanny passed her talent to Daddy and he passed it on to me!" That is the treasure of continuity.

One day Kip came in, sighed, and wistfully said, "Mom, I really wish I could play the keyboard."

"You can," I assured him.

He looked at me in astonishment. "No, I can't. What do you mean?"

"I mean I know you can play the piano if you decide you want to. After all, I play the piano. Your aunt plays the piano. Both of your grandmothers can play. And your Uncle Tim is a professional pianist. Of course you can play. It's in there in your genes. Just let it out." He believed me. As I said, the concept of family heritage is one of our treasures. He began to develop his talent and became so proficient that he traveled for five years in concert ministry.

TREASURING GRANDPARENTS

A child surrounded with a warm, loving family develops a sense of security which cannot be duplicated by anything else in the world. Recalling my childhood, I remember some of my happiest moments were spent at Granny Holder's house. She was my father's mother. Since she lived right down the street from us, I popped in at least once a day. Granny always made me feel special and important in the unique way that grandmothers have.

I was concerned about this sense of family closeness for my own son, since Kipling is an only child. With no brothers or sisters, not even any cousins on my side of the family, would he develop that sense of value for family which meant so much to me as a child? Robert and I began to pray about this. Before long, through a miraculous series of circumstances, my father was able to retire. He built a country home just up the hill from us, and he and mother were there for Kip all during my son's developmental years. In fact, Kipling would stop in to visit them every afternoon when he got off the school bus. Daddy let him help tend the baby chicks and gather in the squash. Mother always had warm cookies and milk, with plenty of time for him. Those were special days of bonding in the life of my young son.

If physical closeness is impossible in your family circumstance, you must make a special effort to bridge the generations. Communication is the vital link. In this age of split-second communication tools, the failure to keep in touch is one of the saddest comments on today's family.

Should you write or call? Both! Write and call and record tapes to send and make videotapes. It is always a thrill to hear a loving voice across the miles on the telephone. But letters and tapes can be read or played again and again. Sometimes make a "Grandpa and Grandma Are Great!" poster. Have your children write down all the things they love about their grandparents. Sign it with their pictures and mail it. What a lovely surprise that would be for your folks.

On holidays, the gifts your children make or choose themselves are much more cherished than an expensive package labeled "From All of Us." Encourage your child to share his talents with his grandparents. When your child sends a little gift of shells or finger paintings or paper chains, the grandparents know it was made for them with love. They have received a hug through the mail.

When the grandparents come to visit, encourage them to share those family stories that only they know. Ask them to teach your children their specialty, whether it be whistling, braiding, playing marbles, or carving. Please *connect* during these visits. Do not just sit and watch the latest video.

TANGIBLE TREASURES

As much as possible, have tangible reminders of your family heritage on display in your home. In our bedroom sits an old rocking chair in which my Great-grandmother Barton rocked my Granny Holder as a child. Granny rocked me in that same chair. She gave it to me when my baby was coming, so Kip was also rocked in that creaky old chair. It is not the most beautiful rocker around, but its value is intrinsic.

In a collection of family pictures stands a very special one: the gathering of five generations, taken on the day my baby was dedicated to the Lord. Standing together on the porch of Granny's house are myself holding Kip, my dad Jofred Holder, his mother Ethel Holder, and her mother, Bessie Barton. What a treasure! Not many families have five living generations at one time.

Another treasure of that day was the fact that the very same pastor who dedicated me as a baby, Brother Bob Caddell, did the honors for my tiny son in the same church where I grew up, where I knew I belonged.

TREASURE A PERMANENT CHURCH HOME

That brings us to another very important point. Give your family stability and heritage by finding a good church. Get rooted and stay there. Let your children grow up through the Cradle Roll on to

Primary Class, then the Youth Department. Let them walk down the aisle to marry their mate at the altar where they knelt and invited Jesus into their hearts. Let the Body of Believers you belong to nurture them. Please do not be a rolling tumbleweed, here at First Church today, gone to Christian Center tomorrow. Building stability takes time. It takes weathering storms and crises. Build those eternal relationships. Believe me, it is worth all the effort.

Perhaps the opportunity will come for advancement in your husband's career or your own. If it means uprooting your family and moving to another part of the country, please weigh everything very carefully. Pray earnestly. Seek the Lord's direction for your family's life, not the corporation's decision. Money and prestige are very attractive, but at what cost? Will you be required to spend too much time apart from your family? Will your new position be doing something *for* them or *to* them? If your final decision must be to uproot the family, then be sure to build bridges between the new life they must make and the old familiar one. Return for visits as often as possible during the transition time. Allow the family an increased budget for long distance calls to old friends. With your newly increased salary, you can afford it. Ask the Lord's guidance in quickly establishing your family into a new Church Body.

Continuity. Stability. Permanence. These are real treasures of the home. In our throwaway, materialistic world, we need them for our children more than ever before.

TREASURE FURRY FRIENDS

Even pets can bring a sense of continuity to a family. My husband had a grand old mongrel dog, Rex, who came to live at the Summers home when Robert was only six years old. His family history is filled with tales of Rex's mighty exploits, such as the time an embarrassed older brother had to haul raging Rex off the football field when he had tangled with the Bulldog mascot of the visiting team.

Rex was both friend and protector. He saw Robert through all his school years, a devoted canine companion.

Yet I have heard mothers explain airily, "Oh, we had to give Buster away. He wouldn't stay out of the flowerbed." What did it matter that the children grieved over his loss? "They'll get over it. He was just a dog."

In our own home, a tiny ball of fluff we named Shasta came to bless our family when Kip was in the first grade. This delightful cat lived with us for seventeen years. I think God gave her more than nine lives. Acknowledged master of the silent "miaow," Shasta was woven into the tapestry of the Robert Summers family.

TREASURE MEMORIES

Concentrate your concern on the important treasures of your home. Material goods do not really matter in the long run. They do not last. Good memories do. Loving touches do. The circle of happiness matters most of all.

First Lady Barbara Bush put the matter very wisely to the graduating students at Wellesley College, Class of 1990, "As important as your obligation as a doctor, a lawyer, or a business leader will be, you are a human being first, and those human connections with spouses, with children, with friends are the most important investments you will ever make," she declared. "At the end of your life, you will never regret not having passed one more test, winning one more verdict, closing one more deal. You will regret time not spent with a husband, a child, a friend, or a parent. Our success as a society depends not on what happens in the White House but on what happens inside your house." Wise lady. Wise words.

Keep reminders of those happy events which happen inside your house. What special things bring a smile to your face when you see them? Which pictures warm your heart? These are all treasures. Put them out where they will gladden your day, rather than keeping them stuffed in an album or locked away in the attic.

As a child, Kip loved trains. Grandparents and friends always knew what to give him. So he wound up with quite an assortment of locomotives. Of all those many different trains Kip enjoyed, I have kept one old "iron horse" through these years. It now sits on the mantel against the stone fireplace, a reminder of that little boy who brought so much joy into our lives.

Over in the corner of our Hill Country library/den is the wicker elephant which served as Kip's toybox. When I found out I was pregnant, I delightedly acquired that elephant. I brought it home and painted it hot pink, since I was sure my baby would be a girl. I set it up as an announcement in the spare room to say, "This is now becoming a nursery for our little one."

Eight months passed, then our big, healthy *boy* appeared on the scene. My thrilled husband rushed home and tied a bright plaid necktie on that pink elephant to proclaim, "I have a *son!*"

The son is now grown. The elephant is now orange and has a lot in common with the Velveteen Rabbit. It has been loved and used until it is a bit frayed. Its ears have been wired back on many times. Its tusks are loose. Heaven only knows what happened to the plaid tie. But it is stacked full of memories, including all those Dr. Seuss books that we read time and time again.

It waits for the happy day when Kip's two little girls, Mackenzie and Riley, can come discover the treasures inside. Sometimes when I walk by, I give the old thing a brief pat and smile at the memory of Robert's plaid tie. A treasure may come in all shapes and sizes.

Obviously we cannot keep every little memento that comes our way. But there are certain items which will always hold a special significance for your family. Things you will cherish more and more as the years go by.

Attached to a third-grade picture of my son is a note written in childish scrawl on the back of an empty check register. It reads, "To JoAn Summers. From Kip Summers. I love you." He had just begun writing cursive and passed me that note in church. What a treasure.

TREASURES FOR TOMORROW

Kip also liked to draw. He always had a pen or pencil or crayon close at hand. One day in Sunday School, he had listened to the story closely, but he got the message of "Peace, be still," a little mixed up. (See Mark 4:35-41.) During the church service, he drew a picture of Jesus standing in the bow of the boat, hand outstretched against the stormy sea, saying "Please—be still!" Robert loves that memory. Sometimes when the tumult of pastoral involvement gets a bit much, he recalls his son's interpretation of Christ's words, "Please. Be still."

Another time I convinced Kip that he could draw an illustration of my story as I told it in Children's Church. With liquid crayons on a big sketch pad, he made Danny Duck come alive for those children. He was only ten years old at the time. This gave him a real sense of participation in our ministry. I was so delighted with the results that I had the sketch framed, and dear old Danny Duck still hangs in my office. Later on, as he continued to sketch for me when I taught at Children's Camps, I gave his sketches away as prizes for the child who needed a special award.

TUCK AWAY THE TREASURES

The important thing is to recognize the treasures around. Don't toss them out and regret the loss later on. Young mothers often get so caught up in just daily coping that they forget these are the years of memories in the making. Keep a stack of those drawings your budding artist created. You can sort through them later and pull out the best. Tuck away some of the most special baby clothes. The lacy cap your baby wore at her dedication can be kept through the years until her wedding. How special for her to carry it as "something old" when she walks down the aisle to meet her groom.

Put back a favorite toy or doll your child has outgrown. Be sure to keep in your library those favorite books you read aloud at bedtime. Save that special bunny she cuddled when she slept. Give away things that don't matter, but keep the treasures.

Photographs are sometimes great treasures. I tend to like the casual pictures caught at happy times, rather than the formal, posed studio shots. I remember my Grandmother Darst's house being totally covered with family pictures. She hardly had any wall space clear. Pictures of her loved ones were everywhere she turned. The older I grow, the more I understand. Pictures are memories. A frame holds a fragile moment in time. Seeing it transports you back to that happy event, brings a smile, lightens the heart.

We have pictures sitting around of those who have gone on before us into their reward. Though they stepped across time into eternity, they remain with us in the picture—Daddy or Granny or Johnnie Lee. We know that as we have been together here, so we will meet them again on the other side. Until then, their pictures are treasures which keep their memory close.

TREASURES AND SIGNIFICANCE

It is important to keep such treasures of the past and to teach our children their significance. That gives them a feeling of continuity. "Great-grandpa carved this whistle long before you were ever born. See how clever he was at making things with his hands—just like you are. That's your family heritage from him." Link your child with the goodness of his past as well as pointing him to a bright future.

Kipling's Great-great-grandmother Barton pieced together a happy kind of quilt for him when he was born. She was eighty-five years old at the time. It is an antique pattern of colorful turtles with a bright red backing. She was not able to do the quilting before she died, so I am completing this family treasure. As I hold it in my hands, quilting the tiny stitches, I think how this piece of needlework began with a lady who was born in the mid-1800's. Now I am completing it, a lady born in the mid-1900's. My son began his family with Mackenzie

Grace in 1995. Little Riley arrived in 1997. As this quilt cuddles and covers my precious granddaughters, it will be stretching across six generations and three centuries. Now that is family continuity!

Along with past treasures, it is also important to keep treasures of the present. Ask the Lord to help you recognize a treasure and hold onto it. Learn to see the significance of things. My friend Jan says, "That's one reason I love you, Jo. You see meaning in *everything.*"

Since we have only one life, I believe we need to make it count for as much as possible. We ought to truly enjoy all the richness of meaning that the Lord brings across our path.

TRAVELS AND TRIALS

To see the pastel drawing of irises hanging in our breakfast room, you would never realize its great value. It is a treasure from the summer of 1989, when Robert and I took a missionary journey to Poland and Czechoslovakia with our spiritual son John. This was just before the walls of communism began to fall. In fact, we were in Poland when the government turned over. We arrived in Czechoslovakia the day after the freedom demonstrations began. It was quite a providential time to be there in ministry. It was also nerve-racking to be followed and watched all the time.

We travelled long, tiring days over winding roads, behind sputtering tractors and horse-drawn carts. We were questioned by stone-faced border guards who searched our belongings. We held our breath, praying, lest they find our Bibles and teaching notes.

The morning of our last day on the road we were served breakfast at the home of a Polish pastor. The date was August 14, my birthday. I was so weary that I hardly cared. I felt a million miles from my home and roots. After our meal, Pastor Kornelius sat down at his piano and began to play an American song he knew. "There's room at the cross for you . . ." he sang. It was a tender, special moment when

God's presence was near.

Later that day, after more hours of travel, we finally arrived at the camp where we were to speak. The region was gripped in a heat wave, and there was no air-conditioning to be found. After settling into our quarters in a 200 year old farmhouse, we walked down to dinner at the campground. The dining room was in an ancient country place which was in process of being restored by the church people. There were no screens on the windows, so flies by the thousands roamed at will. At least two hundred of the nasty little bugs were crawling all over the food set out on the table before us. Self-pity peeped through the window of my heart's door as I thought, *Happy Birthday, JoAn. Nobody here even knows or cares that this is your special day.*

From the corner of his mouth Robert coaxed, "Dish your food out from the bottom of the bowl." Right.

The Polish brothers and sisters were fascinated by their American guests. So not only did I have to fight the flies off my food, I had to do it with the whole dining room full of people staring at me in wide-eyed wonder. They had long since given up the battle against flies, because they had no insecticides nor other means to fight. There I sat before them, eating with my right hand and shooing flies with my left. Surely a fascinating sight.

A BLESSING TO TREASURE

Finally that meal was over. Chattering in Polish, the ladies all rose from the table, cleared the dishes, and went into the kitchen. Suddenly I heard the sound of singing—and I could understand the words!

"Hahpie Burzday to you, Hahpie Burzday to you—

They came out carrying a lovely cake, lighted candle glowing in the center.

"Hahpie Burzday, Zjoanna, Hahpie Burzday to you."

It was the sweetest rendition of the birthday song I have

ever heard. Not one of those ladies could speak English, but they had learned that song in my language to bless me. They gave me a bouquet of cockscomb flowers tied with ribbon. They presented me with the framed pastel drawing of irises by Beata, one of the artists in their congregation. Then the leader of the camp prayed a Polish blessing over me. What a birthday! John had planned the whole event months in advance when he was there on his last trip. They had pulled it off beautifully.

Instead of that day being the birthday everyone forgot, it turned out to be an incredible, unforgettable treasure.

LAY UP TREASURES IN HEAVEN

Life is made up of celebrations and crises, highs and lows, held together by the bonding of daily routine and ritual. For a good balance, acknowledge your past, make the best of your present, and lay up treasures in Heaven for your future.

Jesus told us, "Lay not up for yourselves treasures upon earth, where moth and rust doth corrupt, and where thieves break through and steal: But lay up for yourselves treasures in heaven, where neither moth nor rust doth corrupt, and where thieves do not break through nor steal: For where your treasure is, there will your heart be also." (Matthew 6:19-21 KJV)

How do we lay up treasure in Heaven for our future? We all know that when we leave this life we can take nothing with us. It is what we do with our time now that matters.

Here are some treasures we can lay up in Heaven: Faithfulness to the Lord. Integrity of heart. Honesty in our dealings with mankind. Love for our friends and family. Gifts and offerings to support the ministry of the Kingdom. Souls we have led to the knowledge of Christ. A life lived by the principles laid out for us in the Word of God.

"When the Son of Man comes in his glory, and all the angels

with him, he will sit on his throne in heavenly glory. All the nations will be gathered before him . . . Then the King will say to those on his right, 'Come, you who are blessed by my Father; take your inheritance, the kingdom prepared for you since the creation of the world. For I was hungry and you gave me something to eat, I was thirsty and you gave me something to drink, I was a stranger and you invited me in, I needed clothes and you clothed me, I was sick and you looked after me, I was in prison and you came to visit me.'

"Then the righteous will answer him, 'Lord, when did we see you hungry and feed you, or thirsty and give you something to drink? When did we see you a stranger and invite you in, or needing clothes and clothe you? When did we see you sick or in prison and go to visit you?'

"The King will reply, 'I tell you the truth, whatever you did for one of the least of these brothers of mine, you did for me.' (Matthew 25:31-40)

A life well-lived in caring and service for our King is the best way I know to lay up treasures on the other side. May God give you strength and grace to follow His purpose for your life.

I can assure you that when you follow His purposes, you will discover delightful surprises awaiting you at every turn. After all, Jesus promised that He came to bring us life "to the full." (John 10:10) The Giver of all good gifts has your name on a whole treasure trove of meaningful life events. Sometimes you are not even aware of it until later, until you look back and see just how far you have come by His grace.

This astonishing revelation burst upon me one day in a most unlikely place: Epcot Center at Disneyworld. Robert and I had gone there for a day of fun and relaxation. I was not expecting to see God's guiding hand in my life—but suddenly there it was! Right before me.

If you have been to Epcot, you know that it has many of the most famous places of the world replicated in a smaller form. When we entered the exhibit on France, we sat down and watched the video tour of that great country. As pictures of Mt. San Michele and the

Eiffel Tower sailed by, I turned to Robert and said, "We've been there." We smiled at one another, remembering our lovely times in France.

Then we walked over to the exhibit on Germany, with the beautiful Hummel figurines on display. Once again we saw pictures of places we treasured in our hearts. Again the comment, "We've been there too. And there!"

It happened over and over. Now the majestic Canadian Rocky Mountains. Now flower-filled Guatemala, the land of eternal spring. All these wonderful places that people were trying to experience here at Epcot Center, Robert and I had actually traveled to and ministered in the real world. The Lord had gone before us to fill our lives with such experiences and friends and memories that we had never even imagined when we set out upon our life together.

Our Heavenly Father is so good! His hand of blessing is always filled with new delights for us. His mercies are new every morning. His faithfulness is beyond imagining. All that He asks is that we come "home" to Him, the greatest Treasure of all.

The End